The Nifi

a true story

Linda Fagioli-Katsiotas

ISBN: 10:0989219410
ISBN: 13:978-0989219419

To my children, Nikki and Thomas,
for you to understand who you are.

And to my best friend, Nick,
for your support and patience.

And in loving memory
of Paraskevi (Chevi) Lykas-Katsiotas
One of the strongest women I've ever met.

Circa 1926 – July 5, 2013.

The word "nifi" is a Greek word
used to describe the woman who marries into a family.

PREFACE

Over a period of thirty years, my mother-in-law, Chevi, told the stories of her life. I learned of them first through the translation provided by my husband and then in later years through the simple Greek she used as I began to learn the language.

We often sat in the shade of a giant mulberry tree as she handed me those tiny pieces of the past, pieces that were filled with heartache and betrayal. She told and retold the same stories as if she were tracing the lines of a picture, pressing it into existence. I think Chevi really liked me. I had brought her son back to her after a long absence and I believe she knew I would be a reliable person to whom she could tell her story, a person who would bring it to life.

In 2010, I started writing her stories down but I never expected them to become a book. I only wanted to give her what she wanted, to be sure those who came after her knew that she existed and would know what her life was really like, not the romantic picture or the blatant lies that some were making of it.

In the summer of 2012, those stories began looking like a book. And as it began to unfold onto my laptop, I would realize there were chunks of time missing or one event didn't coincide with the timeline of another so I'd run across the courtyard from my house to hers and ask her a question regarding a detail, a person's name or a date, and then I'd run back and add it to the story. I thought I'd have plenty of time for those questions, for her clarification.

In 2013, the book was finished and I brought Chevi her copy. I was so excited as I made the journey from Long Island to Margariti with the book safely packed inside a suitcase. I would present it to her, put it in her hands, the tangible product of those warm evenings. I knew she'd be tickled. I could picture her keeping it in her black apron and showing it to her neighbors as she made her daily treks to the farm. It didn't matter that it was written in English. She wouldn't have been able to read Greek, either. But I knew she'd like it.

CHAPTER 1

The bus pulled away from the side of the road and I was left there in the village of Margariti, standing next to Nick, my new husband of sixteen months. We had married secretly in the Suffolk County courthouse back home, after knowing each other for a year — my parents still reeling from the shock as we announced that we'd be going to Greece for an indefinite amount of time.

Powdered with the dust created by the wheels of the retreating bus, I watched through strands of sweat-stained hair as the hum of its engine drifted further and further until the bus became a speck in the distance. And then there was only the sound of cicadas, deafening in the midday silence. It was the summer of 1983. My first trip outside of the U.S. I was twenty four years old, inexperienced, uneducated and filled with senseless romanticism. Ready to meet my new in-laws.

The road was deserted, except for an older man across the street, holding the handles of a wheelbarrow but frozen in mid-step. He brought one hand above his eyes, shielding them from the sun, and then watched us for a few seconds. The cart suddenly dropped from his other hand and he sprinted toward us, recognition in his eyes. He and Nick were hugging and kissing, talking wildly, but I understood nothing. It had already become clear to me on the ten-hour, cigarette-filled flight of Olympic

Airlines that the book, *Greek Made Easy*, I had bought back in Queens, New York, and studied for months, was useless and grossly misleading.

I looked longingly down the road at where the bus had disappeared as Nick continued his boisterous reunion with someone who was obviously a close family member with all the emotions flowing between them.

But panic began to threaten my facade of calmness. I needed to somehow relieve myself, preferably with a toilet—one that was enclosed in a bathroom. The bus had passed through numerous quaint little villages with lovely cafes along sharply turning roads, on our eight hour trek north, and then had stopped at an isolated café, far from civilization, with flies nibbling at the food, having first made a stop at the holes behind the cafe that were used for toilets. I wouldn't be able to hold it in much longer.

"Who is this?" I hoped my voice would remind them that I was there.

"This is my neighbor."

Nick gave me a proper introduction of which I understood nothing, so I smiled and accepted the kisses and handshake.

We three walked—gift-laden suitcases in hand—down the dirt path toward *home*. But apparently, my mother-in-law, Chevi, had been meeting every bus from Athens for the past week, anxious to finally reunite with her first born after having been separated for six years. And having heard the departure of the bus, she and two of my sister-in-laws were running toward us.

Anastasia was the first to reach us, her eyes wet with tears. She put her hands to her brother's face as if to be sure he were not an apparition. The two other women followed and many words were exchanged. Much smiling, tears and touching.

I remember Margariti as a place of muted color. The surrounding mountains were naked with different shades of brown and an occasional tuft of brush sticking up from the bald surface. The houses were piled like a broken staircase up the side of the mountain, their red roof tiles shining with the reflection of the sun. And higher up, walls of fallen gray stones, from the ruins of time, lined the ridges of brown as the mountain ascended upward into the blue cloudless sky.

And my in-laws' house.

It stood on a small hill of dirt. Mammoth stork nests sat atop its roofless structure of gray stone and wild unkempt grape vines grew into the unprotected windowless window frames. A full stairway made of large crooked stones went up the side of the house and stopped at the second-floor entrance of the structure. The fact that, all but one room was without a roof, and the bottom floor was uninhabitable, was explained with a brief comment about a fire that had occurred twenty years before. At the foot of those stairs was a smaller, two-room house, which is where we would spend the next two months, and I would try—but never succeed—to acclimate myself to the pests that came in the screenless windows, the bats that had taken residence in its roof, the spiders that found their way into every crevice, never discouraged by my vigilant destruction of their webs and the flies that were a constant buzzing nuisance until dark—which is when the mosquitoes took over that role.

I don't remember seeing my father-in-law, Tomas, but he must have been there. I know that Nick's younger brother, Fotis, was in the army and we wouldn't see him until the end of the visit. His married sister, Vaso, lived a few miles away in Igoumenitsa and we would visit her at the hospital after the birth of her first child, in the following month, and it would be years before we would find out that she had never received any of the wedding money we had sent her through Tomas. But sisters, Anastasia and Eftihia—though they lived and worked in a different village, enjoying an unprecedented amount of freedom for young village women of that time—seemed to be with us all that summer. They would cart our dirty laundry off to the *vrisi*—the natural spring near town—hand-wash it, sun-dry it and then return it folded. I did go with them sometimes and tried to do it myself, but previously, I'd never in my life hand-washed more than a few light items. This laundry was heavy and difficult. Just trying to lift one water-soaked pair of jeans was a feat, but then to wring the water from it was beyond my physical capability. In the time I could wash those jeans, and I use the term *wash* lightly, the other woman would be finished with their entire load. I felt like a child being kept occupied while the adults attended to a task of importance. Our drinking water also came from the *vrisi*, as there was no indoor plumbing and the well water from the yard could not be trusted. This lack of water made personal hygiene a challenge.

Before Nick was able to construct a makeshift shower by rigging a barrel of water atop the wall in the burned out portion of the house, we *showered* by soaping up and pouring water over each other. I remember enjoying that a great deal. Not because it was an act of intimacy, but rather because it was the only time I was alone with him . . . and I missed having someone to talk to.

The word *privacy* does not translate well into Greek and in those days, the idea was a bit elusive. I suppose it was a harsh life so, between the poverty and the arranged marriages, the idea of a private peaceful moment from others seemed more like isolation, a lonely event. And so, there was always someone between us, being a good host, seeing to our needs and being sure we were never left alone which would have been a terrible insult.

I remember always feeling slightly nauseous. The sunlight was intense. The air smelled of sheep dung and burning wood at all times. Wood fires were used for all cooking so, especially first thing in the morning, the smell was everywhere. The food tasted odd in my mouth. Everyone tried desperately to give me what they thought an American would eat. Meat and Coca Cola. But I've never liked carbonated drinks. And meat? Well, I would have loved a nice hamburger, a porterhouse steak, roast chicken, but the coveted lamb that was killed and cooked for the prodigal son's return was the icing on the cake for my nausea.

My two sister-in-laws worked tirelessly trying to maintain a living space that was welcoming and comforting. I wanted to tell them how grateful I was, but all I could do was smile.

It was Anastasia who held my head and stroked my face when I was weak from the prolonged vomiting that occurred from the poisoning I would get at the bouzouki club. If I hadn't been so shy, I might have told them that the bottle of portokalada tasted a little strange.

But on that first day, Eftihia—strong and beautiful—took my arm and led me into the little two-room house. She spoke to me with her smile and I didn't know then that I was looking at my own daughter as a young woman, as they would someday have so much in common. But at that moment, Eftihia was trying to cushion my shock as I looked around.

I tugged at my husband's sleeve and whispered, "I need a bathroom, Nick." He smiled at the hushed giggles as the women discussed the way I had shortened his name.

I looked around and wondered where they had built the thousand-dollar-bathroom. Nick and I had worked extra hours at the diner and saved relentlessly, turning our earnings into a money order which had been sent with a letter explaining to Nick's father, Tomas, the need for a bathroom for the American bride. But it simply did not exist and I didn't understand the reason for its absence — though in my mind I had pictured a modern, tiled room, complete with a locked door. Perhaps there had been a discussion about it, but not with words that I had understood. I do remember, however, where I was ushered to, as the family listened in awe to their Nikos speaking English.

The family *bathroom* — a small closet-sized room on the second floor, up the uneven stone staircase — had a wide pipe leading to a ditch far below and a spider-filled opening in the wall, one might call a window, next to a porcelain toilet that had been placed over the pipe, a bucket of water waiting, as a means to *flush.*

There is a term that comes to mind as I recall that day: *shy kidney* — which was coined for those who have difficulty doing their business when others are about, and this may have been my problem at that time, with the family waiting outside the rickety wooden door which was held shut by a string. But I tend to think it was the snake skin that I saw embedded between the stones and the realization that snake skins come off of actual living snakes. Consequently, the bathroom issues remained for the entire summer.

As time crept forward and the villagers came to get a look at the American, I did my best to sit, smile, nod and listen to the buzz of incomprehensible conversation. When I would say anything to Nick, all movement would stop as the ever-captive audience would become entranced in the gibberish between us. So — naturally, when a bug was trapped within one of my muffled yawns and I felt it flit about my palate, given the choice of a hacking spit with no hope of explaining my behavior or an unnoticed swallow, I chose the latter. It just seemed more tolerable to me.

"I want to go home!" Tears streamed down my face. I tried to sob as quietly as possible, enclosed in the small room, Nick's sisters on the other side of the door. We'd been there less than a week.

"Okay, We'll go home," Nick said.

He was being pulled between the two worlds, wanting to live them both but also wanting me to love them both as much as he. In the end, it was the sea that had the final say.

We rode the bus to the seaside village of Parga. From the bus window, as we teetered on the mountain edge with each hairpin turn, I saw the hypnotic blueness of the Ionian Sea for the first time. The mountainside continued down into the shimmering turquoise, revealing rocky edges of underwater cliffs as if they were only inches from the surface. And patches of changing shades of blue slowly became black as they descended into the depths.

It was love at first sight. If all else had been pushing me to leave, run, get out as fast as I could, this one sight ensnared my heart and I knew I would stay. I had grown up on Long Island and had a variety of seaside fun at my disposal: the wild Atlantic Ocean, the calm salty bays, and the east end with the lush Hamptons on the south shore and quaint beaches of the north.

But they were completely ruined for me that day.

The untouched beauty was enough to hold me there that summer, but the warmth of that crystal water as I submerged myself into its welcoming embrace, was the seductive siren that continued to call me back over the years. That coastline, in the northern region of Greece known as Epirus, offered pristine beaches that were often deserted. At that time, and for many years afterwards, that particular area was the poorest and least visited by tourists, which was the reason for my simultaneous misery and joy. That day, I bathed in the warmth of the Ionian and the nausea washed away. I had Nick all day, someone to talk to and share the beauty with. I was renewed.

But each beach visit ended in Margariti. On the return bus ride, I felt my throat tighten, my heart quicken and braced myself for the evening. Cars were rare back then, so we would walk into town when the heat subsided after sunset. The main street was packed with people, sauntering back and forth, stopping to gossip, visiting with friends or relatives in the houses on the way.

We were no different. Many had heard about Nick's return and stopped us as we walked. The cafés and taverns were filled with men, a wreath of cigarette smoke hugging their heads. It seemed everyone was a talker with very few listeners. They had loud excited voices, their faces animated, their hands gesturing with large exaggerated movements. I was sure there'd be an altercation of some kind. Chairs were flung aside, shirts grabbed across the table and then . . . hugs, kisses and hearty slaps on the back.

"They're just saying hello," Nick explained. "Most of these guys live outside of the country – in Germany. I'm the only one that went to America . . . well, there was that other guy, Louie's brother. We visited him in Manhattan, remember? But we were the only two . . ."

I nodded. I remembered, but I didn't yet know Nick's friend, Louie, and the old man we had visited in Manhattan, was just that . . . *some old guy*. None of these names or faces had much meaning to me yet.

The women strolled back and forth past doors that had big names painted above them such as: hardware store, supermarket, stationery store, butcher, produce seller, bakery. All were packed with their wares in tiny ground-floor rooms of old stone buildings with worn facades. As the women walked in their unhurried pace, some with both hands behind their backs, others holding hands or arm in arm, they stopping to chat but none sat with the men. Conspicuously, I was the only woman sitting in a café when Nick and I would choose a destination. I knew we were breaking some unspoken rule, but my foreign status seemed to excuse me for such behavior. Within moments, the empty chairs at our table would become filled with men; more chairs would be pulled across the square and crowded around us with old friends from childhood, their fathers or brothers, friends of Nick's father or brother and most of them were absently swinging beads through their fingers. I'd learn that they were called *worry beads*, though none who swung them seemed too worried. And the men would talk while minutes became hours. It's not an easy feat to sit for what feels like eternity, understand nothing, and yet nod and smile.

On the walk home, away from the dim lights of the town, Nick would point out the constellations and I would relish those moments, enveloped in the darkness of anonymity. Without streetlights—those would be installed years later—the majestic black sky was peppered with varying sizes of twinkling lights, crowded together. It seemed that no part of the sky was forgotten.

Once back at the house, we had a meal, and as guests or family members went off to bed, my mother-in-law, Chevi, would quietly talk to he son. She seemed to have much to say. She talked and talked.

"What is she talking about, Nick?"

"Oh, just the old days. . ."

I was interested to know about the *old days* and it would take me thirty years before I could understand most of what she was saying, but that night I watched her as she chewed small pieces of her story and waited for her son to translate it for her nifi before the next bite . . . and I was completely mesmerized by her rendition of *the old days*

CHAPTER 2

Senitsa is a small village that lies across the valley from Margariti in the northern mountains of Epirus, south of the Albanian border. This was where Chevi was born to Anastasia and John Lykas in 1926.

Young Anastasia slid in and out of consciousness as she lay on the damp mat in the corner of the tiny room. The midwife at her side tried to prop her up, to create a more effective birthing position by pushing a rolled woolen blanket to the small of her back.

"Leave that now. It does no good." Anastasia's mother-in-law, Vasiliki, spoke to the midwife as she brushed the matted hair from her nifi's face. "Put your weight behind her."

The midwife pushed Anastasia's shoulders, getting her halfway between reclined and sitting, "Up you go, child." She slid her body behind the girl, and looked at Vasiliki,

"When the next one comes, you push down here." She pointed to the space between the girl's breast and the mound of her belly. "The little one needs help."

Their voices, like the hollow wind pushing into the emptiness of a cave, barely reached young Anastasia through the haze. She stared at the wooden slats of the ceiling and floated upward, toward them, vaguely aware of the flies buzzing somewhere in the small spaces of the room. The ancient beams swallowed her.

Slowly. Up. And then she was home. Her mother's hair. The scent of rosemary and thyme. Sweet melodies from her sister, stirring by the fire—then pain, sharp and cutting, and she was back in the house of her husband—someone was pulling her body apart. She was lost in the stupor of half sleep from the exhaustion that comes from hours of labor.

"Push!"

The older women tried to help the young girl, but she lay staring at the wood above, growing quieter. Her face contorted in intervals of pain, her body rising with each convulsive movement. And just as it was decided that she would be unable to help anymore with the child's delivery, the infant emerged from between her bloodied thighs—first the head, gently rotating in the hands of Vasiliki, then the shoulders and then she was there. Baby Chevi. She took her first breath in the arms of her *yiayia*—her grandmother. And Yiayia Vasiliki, wiping the infant with a clean cloth, felt a flood of relief with the baby's first cry, signaling a living child. John heard that cry and bolted into the room to greet his newborn son, the man's red hair falling into his eyes as he swung around to get a look.

"A girl," he sighed. Then he turned and left the room.

Chevi's young mother never quite regained her strength. She lingered for a few months until she finally found rest in the Senitsa cemetery. Her parents blamed John for their daughter's death and never came to see the child. Chevi would not know anything of her mother's family until she was an adult and became acquainted with some of her mother's cousins shortly before her wedding day. And so it was Yiayia Vasiliki who took over as caregiver to her new granddaughter while John went about the task of finding a new wife, preferably one who could give him sons.

Wife number two gave birth to Chevi's little sister, Ioanna a few years later and was buried along side Anastasia before Chevi's second birthday, leaving John's mother with one more little girl to look after. Wife number three came a few years later from behind the far off mountains. Her brothers brought her, traveling all day with her belongings on the back of a donkey, delivering her to her husband's village, as was customary. She was but a child, leaving behind the faces, smells, customs of her own isolated home, and it was not easy, but she knew what was expected.

Days after the wedding, the new nifi fought the edges of the mountain path to find the village water. The old women at the well, eyed her carefully and whispered of a family curse. They spoke about it in hushed voices—with a pretense of secrecy, something that had no existence in any small village—and they knew she heard.

"Someone's jealousy has brought the evil eye . . ."

"and now his children are destined to be motherless."

"Shhh . . ."

The young bride filled her wooden container slowly with the cold water. More whispers and sympathetic looks and with three fingers together, the others touched their foreheads and chests, making the sign of the cross as she passed nearby. And as she walked along the gravel path near the graveyard, afraid to breathe, to move her eyes in its direction, the raised stone markers seemed to grow ever larger as a paralyzing fear gripped her and she realized what she needed to do.

Later, the old crones croaked, "po po po," shaking their heads under their black scarves. "A married daughter returning to her father's home! Such a disgrace on the families. She is ruined."

And so John, accepting his fate: two daughters to raise, and only his tired mother to help, took his usual course of action for solving problems that plagued him. He went to the taverna to discuss it with the other men, over a glass of milky white ouzo and water.

At the same time, Yiayia Vasiliki climbed the path to the church to light a candle, two little girls trailing behind her.

"Virgin Mary, help me," she whispered between taxing breaths, one hand holding a thick branch like the staff of a shepherd pressing it into the earth, helping her up the incline— each step threatened by rocks jutting from the dusty path.

The grey stones of the church sat with authority beside an overflowing almond tree. From the rocky ridge, it overlooked small walls of stone and tiled roofs—the houses that dotted the mountain side. A small square plateau below, formed from cobblestones that were worn to shiny plates by the feet of many generations, held the village water in a large round well, protected by a wooden cover. And far below that, the naked valley was crisscrossed with shades of brown, waiting patiently for the rain clouds that circled the mountain tops, but seemed to always neglect the valley. *The cursed land*, some called it.

Mirrored on the opposite mountain, across the brown expanse, sat Senitsa's sister — Margariti — the stately village with a town hall, a school, a medical center, a police station and a main road passing by, taking with it the young men in search of work to sustain the lives of their loved ones, who waited with impatience for evidence of their success.

For little Chevi, looking out across that sun-burnt valley, Margariti was a village that could be visited instantly with her eyes but as she would later learn, forty minutes by foot and twenty, when she found the *short-cuts*. And, this was the valley — her valley — in the arms of these two villages, that formed the broken cocoon where she would live out her life, never to grow wings, never to fly.

Yiayia Vasiliki taught her girls all she knew about the mountain plants — the fruit that looked like small apples but were poisonous and could kill you with one bite, the leaf that could be pulverized to stop an itch. She knew what could be boiled for headaches, for monthly cramps, and the black seeds of the poppy that could be put into tea to make a person sleep for three days.

And she showed them — as soon as their tiny fingers could grip the wooden dowel — the smooth rotating movements for pressing the dough into thin paper for the pies.

"Sprinkle a little more flour; don't let it rip."

And collecting the olives, "We'll press them into oil and use the old oil to make soap."

"And never leave any behind. Pick every olive, every bean, every onion, every fig". . . as insurance against the hungry times. Then she showed them how to preserve: to tie the onions and garlic in a braid and hang them from the ceiling with the figs and pomegranates, olives in salt water, corn pulled from the husk and stored in sacks with wheat and beans in the cellar — the room dug into the earth in the back of the house.

She showed the girls how to tie a bundle of wood, to sling it onto their backs and to walk stooped over, making their backs flat, like a cart, and with time their spines would grow accustomed to it and straightening to stand would be with effort.

School was not necessary. The girls' labor was needed elsewhere, but Father Lou, pestered the villagers to enroll their children, even the girls. John met the subject with indifference. As long as he felt neither hunger nor thirst, and his clothes seemed to be clean, his winter nights alit with the warmth of the collected wood in the fire, he did not look past the top of his ouzo glass. But Yiayia Vasiliki was different. She was quietly aggressive in her efforts with Chevi and school—and one might assume that this old woman, having endured an arduous life, illiterate, uneducated, controlled in every aspect by the men around her, would be first in line to register her granddaughters with the hope of their breaking free of the village yoke, but such an assumption would only be made by a person who had never lived in that time or place, as she used every bit of her intelligence and cunning to avoid the priest for quite some time and then to articulate long and unlikely scenarios—that one might call lies—as to why her son had not come to register Chevi yet.

"Oh, John is tending to the sheep, on the mountain," she'd say, knowing he never had nor ever would have animals, or "Chevi is visiting my sister in Paramithia," when Chevi was not far behind her on the path and Yiayia had no living sister. But the priest was accustomed to being put off this way. Apparently, it was proper village etiquette to make an excuse that was obviously false, in order to achieve a goal, but to also—at all cost—avoid the unacceptable behavior of hurting one's feelings because, after all, in a small village, the occupants would be living close together for a long time. Better to be talked about for a flimsy excuse than for cruel behavior. So, for example: if one were to have an unwanted guest whose stay appeared to be for an undefined amount of time, the more appropriate response to such a situation would be to say something like, "I'm sorry you'll have to stay in the goat shed *(knowing this would create the hoped-for result)* because the priest needs his brother to stay here for a while," rather than saying, "your digestive habits are making me sick and you've been here a month already; take a hike." And mind you, there is a chance that the visitor would actually move to the goat shed and see that no guest arrives, but the house would be rid of him and he would not mention it. Goal achieved—village etiquette intact.

So Yiayia Vasiliki did her best to keep Chevi free from the shackles of this façade called *school*. She was of the opinion that having Chevi sit in a two room school house wasting time with fifty other children of all ages, would only give the appearance of being educated because she suspected very little learning actually occurred there, which in turn would limit her granddaughter's ability to find a husband. And, besides that, in all likelihood Chevi—because of her old age of ten—would be used to assist the teacher with the unruly smaller children, most of whom had never sat quietly in a chair with a writing tablet or a pencil. But eventually, Father Lou got most of the signatures that he needed by buying a round of drinks at the taverna and Chevi found herself sitting uncomfortably among the first graders in a corner of the school house.

"Chevi Lykas, read this page before the wolves come down from the mountains and eat you."

The teacher was a man, who in her aged memory was as tall as the ceiling, with a voice that boomed like thunder, and with small black weasel-like eyes embedded in a head as hairless as a turtle's shell. He was a man who found it easy and comfortable to use her for creating light moments of fun in the classroom. And the other children laughed as she stared at the lines that were supposed to be words. But it was Greek and she only knew Albanetika, the village dialect—but not its writing.

She endured one full year like this until Uncle Spyros came to rescue her.

CHAPTER 3

On that first visit, I had expected Margariti to be a quiet place because I'd heard it said — though I'm not sure where — that the countryside is peaceful. But this is completely untrue. The cacophony of insect songs intermingled with random outbursts from farm animals like chickens, roosters, donkeys, horses, sheep, and goats, which were kept in yards like family pets. And those animals competed with the clacking sounds of the storks' beaks and the varying pitches of different birds that sailed through the air while a variety of other wildlife screeched and cawed. Eventually they would all become an unnoticed buzz in my daily routine, as familiarity weaved its veil, but in those first days, they mixing together to produce one unending noise at a volume only a newcomer would notice.

As it turns out, roosters will often announce the onset of morning long before light peaks into the valley. And though I had naively believed owls to produce a short melodic *"hoot – hoot,"* Margariti's owls were actually more like a woman's blood-curdling scream. That screech would pull me from my sleep — heart pounding and eyes wide.

"No one is being murdered . . . go back to sleep," Nick would say after being roused by an elbow in the side.

The sheep were different. They sounded like an old man's deep and throaty well-articulated "baa. . . baa" — so much so, that I had

15

to see their mouth movements synchronized with that sound, before I would believe that some older man was not outside the window making sheep noises.

"That's how they sound," Nick chuckled and shook his head — watching me as I stood with my hands on my hips, eyes squinted, looking out the window, studying a dozen sheep in the fading summer light.

"She never had animals when we were growing up." He joined me at the window.

We were looking at Chevi's sheep. Every morning she walked them to the farm, stayed with them while they grazed, milked them, and then returned them in the evening to the yard next to the house. She turned their milk into fresh cheese and yogurt. In later years, she would trade them for goats that she would keep in a goat shed on the farm, but still in her eighties, she would continue the routine. None of her children would end up living in the village — an unusual circumstance in that culture — so she would tend to her animals, and they, with their never-ending needs, would provide her with a sense of purpose and freedom.

But that year, her eldest son and her American nifi, not yet having become parents, still children, ourselves, did not understand this need. So, the sheep with the constant barrage of flies that accompanied them, resided outside our bedroom window and in the morning, quite early, as the storks in their precariously placed nests, loudly clacked their beaks in greeting, we would groan as Chevi called her sheep together and led them away to the farm.

With the mountains picked clean of any buffering trees, the sound waves traveled unobstructed for miles, and any happenings within the valley, sounded like they were occurring in the next room. But, those obstacles to a good night's sleep always disappeared during the midday siesta, when even the birds did not stir in the heat. So, on non-beach days — usually the weekends — as the afternoon breeze rolled off the mountains and anesthetized the village, I found myself nodding off to sleep, a quiet respite from the village-time-anxiety I seemed powerless to free myself from.

On the weekends, guests arrived all day and all evening. Some stopped by for coffee. Others came for a meal which would be cooked in one of the two *fournos*. The word *fourno* means *oven*, but these ovens were unlike any that I had ever seen. They were large hollow domes of cement with a small opening in the front that was loaded with wood. The wood would burn until it produced the coals for heat and then the food would be roasted or baked. There was one fourno on a small roofless platform upstairs, outside the only room left undamaged from the past fire. The other fourno was behind the house, sheltered by a dilapidated shack. Neither fourno, however, would be used to cook the sheep. Yes, Chevi loved her lambs, but as she would say, "food is food!" So, one of their skinless torsos would be affixed to a spit and hand-turned over hot coals in the yard by volunteers, the blaze of the burning wood, hours before, adding to the intense heat of the day.

There was a mix of friends and family, most of whom I would recognize in later years in the old photos of those gatherings, but at that time, I really wasn't sure who was who. It seemed like Nick had hundreds of relatives. I remember the familiar faces of Nick's sisters, including Vaso with her husband, Christos from Igoumenitsa. And I clearly remember Aunt Evangelini. She was one of Chevi's cousins who came with her husband, Thanasi, to every gathering. She and Chevi seemed to be the best of friends, always laughing and talking in the local dialect. She was a sweet older woman, dressed in the customary black garb: dress, stockings, apron, head scarf. I wondered how they survived in the heat. Her sunbaked face, so innocent, and yet whenever she could, she questioned me about my lack of children when I had already been married one full year. The absence of a mutual language between us did not discourage her, for she seemed to know two English words.

"No baby?" She pointed at me and then Nick and then clasped her hands into a praying position and laid her cheek on them and feigned sleep. My face burned red as I understood what she was asking, but even in English, I had no words. She misread my questioning eyes and continued to pantomime, gyrating forward and back with her hips, saying "Niko. . . Niko," and pointing at me. The other women, though overcome with laughter, seemed to be reprimanding her but Evangelini, a woman barely four feet in height and with an angelic cherub-face, just smiled as she continued her line of questioning.

There was also an older man with no legs, being pushed in a wheelchair. Nick's explanation was vague as to what disease had taken them. But the others wheeled him around on the rocky dirt. It was a terrain that might have discouraged many full bodied seniors, though it did not seem to deter him. Always smiling, he seemed to enjoy the company around him tremendously. It wasn't until years later, looking back on those photos, that I realized it was Uncle Spyros and then, knowing his story, I understood his lust for that day, being attended to by the family he had longed for in his youth.

CHAPTER 4

Only Yiayia Vasilliki recognized her son, Spyros, as he strode up the village path, eighteen years after having been killed in Asia Minor in the fighting that followed the first Great War, his hair white with age and suffering.

Spyros Lykas, like his brothers Apostolis and John, had been a young man when he was sent to fight, but the wars ended, time passed and he did not return to convalesce in the bosom of the valley as his brothers had, though his mother waited and watched, ever vigilant as other young men slowly returned, experience etched in their eyes. And after several years of waiting, his mother had given up hope of ever seeing him again. But there he was, returned to his birthplace — still strong and powerful, tall and clear-headed — a man of middle age. Though he was prodded for details about his *adventures*, he shared very little of his years in captivity, of his procreating for his captor, a powerful Muslim landowner with a large harem, for whom he produced many heirs — sons who, as they grew tall, light haired, and blue-eyed — made it ever more apparent to the landowner that it would benefit him to have Spyros disappear from sight lest family members begin to see the children's resemblance to the land owner's slave. But those years that master and slave had shared, fostered a certain bond, though it was one based on servitude, it was still a bond, and it was worth his life. So upon receiving his freedom, he began his journey on foot, adding another year to his separation from his beloved home, having to travel only in darkness for fear of recapture and most certainly more enslavement. So, after tribulations that only Odysseus could have understood, and therefore he shared with no one, he found himself once again in Senitsa, hoping for the luxury of a quiet life, perhaps a small square of land to seed.

Thus, he received from his father that parcel of land, rightfully his after Mr. Lykas was convinced it was truly his son, back from the bowels of Hades. And he set about tilling the hard earth with the help of his niece, Chevi, who naturally could not attend school when it was for reasons that had to do with the production of food. Chevi could not have been more pleased to meet that uncle she had heard many tales about.

Years passed with the hardship of poverty and conflict. The second Great War, and the fight between Greeks devastated much of the little valley, but for its inhabitants, survival had always been a delicate thread.

Chevi, an unmarried woman, a shaky-legged fawn among hungry wolves, approached her yard one morning, hunched over with the weight of the wood on her back. She did not hear the unfamiliar voice until she was too close to avoid him. A stranger stood with her father within the high walls of the courtyard, but they stopped speaking midsentence as she rounded the corner. She registered their uneasy smiles and knew something was amiss, but what? She wondered. She moved closer and let the wood fall from her back and straightened up to her full height—though it was no more than the mid-stone of the storeroom door—and she met their gaze, looking questioningly from the stranger to her father. The two resumed their conversation but they spoke gibberish.

"He is not from the valley," she thought and dismissed his presence. The smaller pieces of wood needed to be brought to the back room next to the fourno. She loaded up her arms, and walked toward the door, but the stranger stepped into her path and spoke.

Her arms were shaking with the weight and she did not know what this person asked of her and why didn't he just ask her father who appeared to know his language.

"Get out of my way you idiot." Chevi spoke quietly, as he continued to stand in her way and when she moved to the right he tried to clear a path for her to pass but he mistakenly chose to move in the same direction, so they danced back and forth and the wood grew heavier.

"May lightning strike you dead." She cursed him and swept past just as the first cut branches began to fall from her hands and the sound of their crashing to the floor as she entered the cooking room sent her father running in to aid her.

"Father, who is that?"

"No one, Chevi. Pick up the wood and bring it to the cooking pile."

"It is someone, father."

"He is here to buy some wheat."

Well, he's an imbecile, she thought, and wondered where his sacks were and how he planned to cart the wheat away.

John returned to the yard to Pavlos' friend, Tomas. Pavlos had spoken well of him and his bravery during the war. He looked strong and healthy, important features for working the fields and providing grandsons to do the same.

Tomas rubbed his chin. He had liked the look of the man's daughter. And she seemed to be shy. She had spoken so softly, though he had no idea of what she had said; she appeared to be someone he could mold to his liking. Yes, he was interested in this arrangement and he told John as much.

"But what was it she was saying to me John?"

"She said she thinks you are very handsome and will love you as a good wife should."

Tomas smiled, shaking his head slowly, "Yes," he thought, "I *am* handsome."

"There is one condition, though, Tomas," John continued.

"Yes?"

"She must stay in this village. I need her here. You can live in this house with us."

Tomas made a very somber face as if he were contemplating this monstrous deviation from tradition. In fact, he could not have been more overjoyed to hear this news. His village, far from Margariti, hidden high within the mountain peaks, had nothing to offer except bickering between siblings for a small worthless piece of land. In this new place he could reinvent himself as Tomas, the worldly traveler, educated, sophisticated, *handsome* man of the household.

"Well," Tomas hesitated and cleared his throat long enough to seem as though he were sacrificing terribly for this woman, "alright, then." He stuck out his hand and the two men shook and sealed the deal.

*   *   *   *

"Uncle, I cannot marry that man," Chevi whispered, "help me."

She trusted Uncle Spyros, as he had become the only reliable man in her life. It was his advice that had helped her father become the owner of their Margariti house that they were living in. If not for him, they would still be living in the two-room hovel in Senitsa. While father had discussed and planned and philosophized while emptying his glass at the taverna, Uncle Spyros had listened and heard about the possibilities across the valley in Margariti.

The Muslims had fled for fear of retribution at the end of the second Great War, but it was expected that some might try to return, once the dust of the civil unrest had settled. So, each day, across the valley, more Christian names were carved into the doors of the Muslim homes as a sign of new ownership and as insurance against their return. The center of town had been slowly occupied. But there had still been some good structures left on the mountainside.

"Go Chevi, get a home. Mark a cross on the door. People will know it is taken." Those were his words that had sent her on a trek across the valley and up the side of the mountain.

Climbing the steep path of hard dirt, she came across a high stone wall that rose far above her head. Embedded in the wall, sat a large wooden gate with a bronze door knocker fashioned into a hand grasping a sphere—Atlas squeezing the world to a size Chevi could endure. She pushed it open and passed into a hidden courtyard. The house stood majestically within and it dwarfed her father's small dwelling in Senitsa. The bottom floors held the customary storage rooms with rounded ceilings and thick walls. Next to them was the cooking house—a separate structure which housed the round belly of a well-used fourno sitting on a dirt floor. Just outside the cooking house stood an ornate staircase, waiting to take her to the living quarters on the second floor. Its first steps had been created in a flat arch, giving the stairs an elegant rounded look, like half of a wedding cake as it rose toward the wall. It ascended to a small landing where it changed direction and proceeded up to the house entrance where a flat platform with a small overhang contained a water trough for washing. She could see from the foot of the stairs that the door had no mark on it yet so, finding a rock, she walked up the steps, rising above the wall as she went, the brown valley painted before her, witnessing her work as she scratched the cross into the worn wood. If only she could write her name, to be sure, so the others would know. But the Christian cross was enough.

The crude marking erased the lives of the family who had fled months before. Rahim, with his young son, had tilled the fields and prayed to Allah for a fruitful harvest while his wife and daughters attended to the house, well protected within the walled courtyard. His brother had laughed at their labor and sought the promised power from the German soldiers who had occupied the village during the second Great War. He knew that the Muslims were the superior ones and would rule the land of Margariti. They needed only to whisper a few Christian names to the Germans, to insure that power. But Rahim was only interested in feeding his family and making more sons. He had no quarrel with the other villagers. And like all events—significant or inconsequential—an end came to that war; the Germans left and took with them their promise to the Muslims who had betrayed their neighbors. Rahim had to protect his wife and children from the revenge of those who had been wronged. So he and his family, with their few cows, disappeared like the morning mist at sunrise. But the villagers, with their long time grudges between brothers, their petty jealousies between friends, and their neighborhood border disputes of generations, fell prey to a war instigated by others, further plunging the people of the valley into the destruction of a civil war, as the rest of the world treated their wounds and grew stronger. Four years later, shrouded in their black shawls of the dead, the women of Greece emerged. Having completed the task of survival, they sought a better life.

Thus, Chevi had claimed a house. Her father's house. The Christian cross on the door proved it. She pushed the door open and walked from the brightness of the day into darkness. The house was colder than she had expected, and appeared to have no possessions inside, only the sitting platform built next to the fireplace. But leaning in the shadows, a broom made from the soft tassels of a corn plant, reached out to her. Another woman's labor, left behind for the new occupant. Chevi went to retrieve it and to open the shutters for the sunlight, but a sudden movement on the floor caused her to push back against the door frame. A black snake sliced over the wood and struck her ankle. The pain momentarily stopped her. She faltered, then backed out of the house to look at her injury in the daylight.

She would nurse the cut and the pain would subside but she was unable to ease the heaviness in her heart as she turned back to the entrance, once again disappearing into the darkness, setting about to create her new home.

And, only a few years later, she implored Uncle Spyros. "I don't like him. I won't marry him."

"Chevi, you are too old and too poor. This is the best offer you will have. If you don't take it, you'll end up unmarried. Accept your fate properly as a village girl should."

"I don't want to marry anyone. I can take care of myself."

Hadn't she proven her worth during the communist invasion, though perhaps only to herself. The children and women had fled to the mountain heights with the elderly, as the Germans descended on the village. But Chevi had bravely stayed behind with Zizis Pateras, the old farmer who refused to leave before sowing his field. As he lumbered over the dirt with his hand plow, she pushed the seeds into the soil and when a sniper began to shoot the dirt around them, sending bits of earth into the air, she shook with fear, but she did not abandon him.

Old Zizis remained calm.

"Who is that fool, wasting bullets on an old man and a little girl?"

He shook his head and continued forward. Finally, with the last seed in its place, Chevi ran home between random bursts of gunfire and found her house empty. Everyone had ascended into the mountains to hide. It was growing dark, but she had lived her fourteen years among those ancient rocks. She knew every stone, every blade of dry grass and could find her way in complete dark of night, even without a moon, which is what she did. She made her way to the others in the deep cave near the fresh water spring and she believed her strength and endurance were cultivated during those oppressive days in that cave. Didn't that prove she was capable?

But Uncle Spyros had heard a different version of that story, which Chevi conveyed many times as an older woman, years later, with the shake of her head and a faint smile. For days, the villagers had heard conflicting news of the impending communist invasion, and their anxiety wore on them. A distant thunder clap sent them running for cover. The odd bray of a donkey or cluck of a chicken produced omens from the wise old women. The mounting stress slowly seeped into everyday life, with the constant conjectures among the villagers, electrifying everyone's nerves. Some of the older ones—in an attempt to relieve the somber state of anticipation—tried to lighten the mood by teasing the children around them.

"Watch out for those communists! They are after all the socks in the village."

So that evening, after having parted with Zizis Pateras, Chevi had indeed slipped into the darkness and found her way up to the cave, and there had been much relief and a collective sigh from those who were concerned for her welfare when she entered unhurt until she began to pull from her apron pockets all the socks from the house, which she had taken time to collect before escaping. This vision of his niece was probably the one Uncle Spyros held when she implored him to remember her competence during the invasion.

Chevi continued her plea.

"Please Uncle, I can farm and sell my goods the way father does. I can take care of myself. I don't need to marry him." She tried to sound confident, using a tone she had often heard her father use while bargaining the price of his wheat.

Uncle Spyros shook his head.

"Chevi, do you see the stork nests on the houses?" He pointed to the top of the neighbor's chimney where two white storks stood among the intertwined twigs of their giant nest.

"Yes, Uncle."

"When I was young, my friends and I would watch the baby storks learn to fly. The mother taught them to fly out of the nest and then fly back. Sometimes, a weak one would try to fly out before he was ready and he would fall to the ground."

Uncle Spyros continued, "Well, my friends and I would play with that little bird on the ground. We poked it with sticks, pushed it around in the dirt, pulled its feet off and then left it to die."

Chevi gasped.

"My dear niece, what I am telling you is this. In a mountain village such as ours, a woman is a baby bird without wings. She is meant to stay in a nest. Your father will get old and die and then you will be left alone like the bird that fell to the ground."

*   *   *   *

A few months later, in her twenty-fifth year, a full decade after many of her peers had married, John gave his daughter to Tomas, saving her from the shame and abuse of being an unmarried woman. It was a somber day. Chevi spent most of it wiping tears from her eyes.

As she entered the church and saw Tomas waiting patiently at the altar, a villager whispered to her.

"I know that man, Tomas, he fought with the communists in the war . . . Yes, I'm sure. That's him."

Chevi suddenly felt the smallness of the church — the walls seemed to crumble, its floor to buckle.

"Communist!" she released the word in an exhale. She knew all about communists. They were to be feared — kidnappers of children — heartless, evil beings. She looked up at her father as he took her arm. Surely, he could not have known. He would never have allowed a communist in his house. She would tell him. But first she should run away. She looked around. All the relatives were there, smiling at her — watching. Many had travelled from far away. She was being slowly led to the altar, her father's eyes straight ahead leading her to the communist like a compass needle drawn north, a smiled pasted on his face. The priest stood waiting.

The priest! She would tell him instead. He would chase the communist from his church. Her heart thundered in her chest as she walked past her relatives and she wondered at their calmness. And then she was at the altar, next to the communist who stood small and unassumingly under an overgrown mustache, ready to receive his prize. Chevi, legs shaking, took her place as her father deposited her and retreated to the back of the church. She kept her eyes riveted to the floor, barely able to breathe, trying to keep herself steady. She opened her mouth to alert the priest but no words came out. Then there were prayers, and vows before God, the wedding crowns exchanged, the priest leading them around the altar. And then it was over. She was the wife of a communist! Arm in arm, they walked down the aisle toward the door. As they left the church, she could stand it no more. She ran to her father.

"Yes, I know," he told her, "but you do not know what that means." So, he explained it to her.

It was true—a common practice during the civil war—a matter of survival, especially in isolated villages like that of Tomas. Families would send a child to fight with whichever party took power in one's village. Tomas' mother made the decision that he was the child that could be expended and so, Tomas waffled between the republican army and the communist army, depending on which took power, at any given time—his family kept safe as they were perceived as loyal, having a child fight for the *cause*. He needed only to survive until it ended.

As Chevi left her father, Yiayia Vasiliki pulled her aside.

"Chevi, my dear, let us walk to the celebration together." She brushed the young bride's hair under her headscarf and continued to walk, "tonight you will be the wife of Tomas. You must obey him. Do you understand?"

"Yes, yiayia." Chevi had no idea what her grandmother was referring to but they spoke no more and continued to the celebration in silence.

That night, Tomas brought the smell of onions and ouzo into the bedroom where Chevi lay waiting. He stumbled around the room, knocked over her washing bowl, hit his head on the window frame and fell to the straw sleeping mat.

"Wife," his hot breath filled the space between them as his hands, like thorns, felt the warmth of her neck, then slid over her night dress, stopping at her breast.

"No," she whispered. He pushed her against the mat, the back of her head slid from the top and rested on the stone floor.

He fumbled with her night dress, tangled his hands, lost in the bulkiness of the cloth. Pulling, tugging, twisting, he found an opening at the bottom and slid his hands up her legs, the garment folding upward to her waist like an accordion without air. Instinctively, she pushed him with both hands and slid further off the mat. He grabbed one wrist and held her down. His body pressed her back into the straw. She tasted salt as his mouth pushed against hers. With her free hand she grabbed at his face.

"Stop it!" He hissed. "You are my wife."

She understood. She obeyed and laid as still as a stone. His breathing became faster with heavy gasps roaring in her ear.

"I'm dying," she thought as the heaviness of his body pressed the air from her lungs, and a hard bulk moved across her thigh. He pulled her legs apart. Then, there was pain. Her back pressed hard into the straw. He split her in half and filled her with his venom. Then it was over. Tomas' breathing became shallow and Chevi heard a soft snore escape. In the dim light of the room she stared at the moon's reflection off the far wall. She slid from the bed and went to her washing bowl, dipped the ends of a cloth into it and washed the blood away with the cool water. She turned and watched her husband sleep, his chest rising and falling, peacefully.

"I'm his property, now," she whispered. And she entertained thoughts of murder.

In the morning, the sun broke through the shutters with stripes of light across the floor. The smoky scent from the cooking fires hung in the air and mixed with the mist. Tomas sat alone on the sleeping mat—his bed.

"I'm a married man," he pondered. He was amused by the wonder of it. His food would be presented to him. His needs would be met. He would have sons for the hard labor of life in the village. A smile broke across his lips. He got up, dressed, and went to the kitchen.

Chevi had been preparing his coffee. As he entered, she quickly swept away bits of grated root laying in crumbled pieces near the coffee pot. She did not meet his gaze as she handed him his morning coffee, her heart hammering in her ears. She held her breath as he took it and eyed him cautiously from across the room as he sipped it slowly.

Abruptly, he put the cup down on the table, his mouth twisted, his nose crinkled.

"I'm going into town," he said.

Then, he rose and walked out. The cup was almost full. He'd barely had any. Chevi quickly poured it into the fireplace and watched as the guilty brown liquid seeped into the ashes. In a flood of relief, she realized she was not a murderess. Months later, when Thitsa came to visit, and grated pieces of a familiar root into a cup of tea to relieve her constipation, Chevi realized that, not only was she not a murderess, she also had not listened carefully enough to yiayia over the years when she explained the medicinal properties of their mountainside and the worst she might have caused Tomas that morning, was a bout of diarrhea.

Tomas spent most of that day at the café in town, being cajoled by the other men and complaining to anyone who would listen about the bitter coffee his new wife made.

Chevi spent the day doing the back-breaking work that was expected of her — collecting water from the well and wood from the mountainside and hauling it up the steep incline to the house for cleaning and cooking. On Saturday, she would load the laundry into a barrel, hoist it onto her back and hike to the spring near the church to do the wash. And now, with Tomas, there was an additional person, more work. She kneaded the ache in her thighs and worried about this new torment that had come with marriage. She rested briefly in the shade of a fig tree. There among the weeds rose the tall dry bulbs of the poppies. She eyed one for a moment, contemplating. Then, she bent and collected a handful of its black seeds. Staring at them in her hand, she wondered, "Were these the same as those yiayia had boiled for father when he was overcome by the dark sickness and needed to sleep?"

How many would she need? She let them fall into her apron pocket.

That evening, she brought her father some tea.

"Tea for you also, Tomas." She spoke to him in his Greek language as best she could and those were the first words she had spoken to him since their awkward dance with the wood, months before, when he had come to talk to John about his daughter.

"Well," thought Tomas, "she's finally warming up to me" and he congratulated himself on his skillful lovemaking which could be the only reason for her sudden thaw. No doubt, the evening chill reminded her of what marvels he had to offer her in the secrecy of the dark.

Chevi put the tray of tea on the table in front of the men. "This is yours, husband." She handed him a cup. She moved to the back of the room slowly, watching. The two men conversed about the days events. Chevi observed Tomas closely. He yawned. His eyelids drooped a bit. He smoothed his mustache and passed gas.

Crash!

Her father's cup fell to the floor as he slumped forward in his chair, snoring loudly.

"*My goodness, that old man falls asleep fast,*" thought Tomas.

"Oh no," Chevi exhaled.

"It's okay; I'll put him in his bed." Tomas heaped the limp body over his shoulder and walked to the bedroom.

In a panic, Chevi rushed to her bedroom, put on several protective layers of bed clothing and laid on the mat. She closed her eyes and feigned sleep, wondering how many hours it would be until her father awoke.

Tomas entered the room. He tilted his chin, scratched his head and looked quizzically at the motionless lump in the bed. Perplexed at the speed at which this family seemed to fall asleep, he went outside to smoke a cigarette in the moonlight.

Chevi had not thought her plan through very well. She had only hoped for her second married night to be a peaceful one. Now she lay in bed far earlier than she had expected to be there, damp with sweat from the layers on her. She needed to relieve herself of her evening tea, and her nervousness did not help matters. She heard Tomas humming to himself, as he entered the house again. She would not be able to sneak by him. Through the wall, she heard the even tremors of her father's deep slumber. Her worry deepened with every passing minute. She thought about wetting the bed. Surely, that would take care of all her worries. Tomas would be appalled and stay away from her and she would have the relief that she was growing desperate for. In the end, she thought better of it. She could not predict how he would react and she might end up more uncomfortable than ever.

She got out of the bed, her hair matted with sweat. She lifted a night shirt over her head, then another, and another. The shuffle of footsteps on the floor startled her and as she turned, pulling her head from the cloth, she stood face to face with Tomas, a wide grin on his lips. He said something about his tool. She did not understand.

"Perhaps he was going to build a tool shed as father had suggested during dinner," she thought. He certainly seemed pleased with the idea.

"I'm going to pee," Chevi said and swept past him, disappearing behind the bathroom door.

Tomas went to the sleeping mat and waited. He heard the splash of water as it was poured from the bucket, flushing over the waste hole, but the door remained closed.

Chevi, turned the empty bucket over and sat on it. The cool air bit through the thin cloth and she thought about the warm layers she had just shed. She waited. Perhaps he would fall asleep. When she felt a reasonable amount of time had elapsed, she opened the bathroom door. Except for the soft snores from the two bedrooms, it was quiet. She tiptoed to the sitting area near the fire and lay down near the dying flame, pulling the discarded night clothes from the floor and wrapping them around her like a bed sheet. Then she tried to sleep, Tomas breathing softly on the sleeping mat beside her. He had waited for Chevi. It was obvious to him that she was excited about having him a second time, which was not surprising at all, as he knew he was a great masculine specimen. But she had taken so long and the bed was so soft . . . and warm.

As it turned out, Chevi did not have to endure his body on hers every night as she had mistakenly believed. If she added some wine to dinner and some ouzo afterwards, she could usually have a peaceful slumber with only the occasional snorts and gargles of his snoring to interrupt her dreams. On the nights that he insisted on his husband entitlements, she found, quite by accident, that if she concentrated on something intently, like planning her day at the market or arranging the vegetables on the farm, she barely knew he was there.

One night, he had come to her stinking of a familiar odor. It filled the bedroom. He rolled on top of her and began his usual pawing and pushing.

Chevi thought, *"what is that smell?"* and with furrowed eyebrows, biting her bottom lip, she closed her eyes and tried with intensity to identify it.

"Chives?" she thought.

With a brief glance at his wife's face, Tomas was secure in his role as master. Bump, bump, thud, the straw mat hit the wall.

"Dill?" she wondered.

Groans from Tomas.

"Garlic?"

Grunt, grunt.

"White onions?"

Gasp, heavy sigh.

"Cabbage!" she thought confidently. *"Yes, that's it."*

Tomas rolled off of his wife, farted loudly, and was asleep in seconds.

"Cabbage," thought Chevi as she drifted to sleep, *"that reminds me . . . I want to give some cabbage to cousin Evangelini for her goats."*

*   *   *   *

The cool air of January signaled the season for picking the olives. Chevi, with a swollen belly, awaited the birth of her first child. Tomas had some urgent business at the village café so she and her father, taking some bread and goat cheese wrapped in a cloth, walked through the valley to their olive grove to unfold the black nets under the olive trees. They hit the branches with sticks, encouraging the little black spheres to fall to the nets. After the olives were collected, John would take some to Dimi at the mill to be turned into oil—the ingredient that was poured thick into all recipes like broth in soup. It was the mother's milk of the mountain that kept them alive when the fields yielded little.

Yiayia Vasiliki and Chevi would store some olives in vinegar and water with sliced lemons to be eaten later and some would be sold at the market with eggs from the chickens and the snails collected after the rains.

On market day, Chevi would go to the seaside village of Parga to sell her wares with the hope of selling enough to return with some needed household items and a few extra drachmas. She went with her cousin, Evangelini. During those cool months, Chevi wrapped herself tightly with her black shawl as she rose before dawn to load the donkey with the goods. Then she and her cousin walked behind the animal, crossing the valley, through Senitsa and over the mountain to Parga. The women arrived in the marketplace before noon and greeted the other women as they set out their wares. They passed their time gossiping with the others from Senitsa.

"Mitsos' dog bit the man who sells cloth. That dog should be brought to the farm and tied up. It is too vicious to be inside the village."

"Yes! That nasty animal scares the devil out of anyone who passes by. He should bring it to the mountain where his goats are."

"He should shoot the ugly mutt."

"That cloth man has a dark heart so the dog bit him; dogs know. It's their nature."

"Yes." said Chevi, thinking about some vicious dogs that had determined her worth once and she said, "Let me tell you about some sheep dogs."

The other women waited. They knew that Chevi was always good for a story and it helped pass the time.

Chevi continued, "Before I was to marry Tomas, he took me to his village, to meet his family. We went by foot and first it took one full day to get to Kanali—you know, that town near the river?"

Chevi did not wait for answers, "I have a cousin there. We stayed there that night and the next morning we started out again for his village. We walked and walked and I asked him, 'Tomas where is your village?' and he said 'it's just over that mountain.' So we walked more. We stopped for water and we ate some bread and cheese that my cousin had given us and we started out again

33

and I said, 'Tomas where is your village?' and again he said, 'it's just over that mountain.' Oh my I had no idea. He was not a person to tell me things straight. We walked for a full day more over so many mountains, and finally we got there and I was so nervous. It was so high up and the houses were on steep paths so one house looked like it was on top of another. The neighbor woman saw me and she told me 'you're marrying into the worst family. Your father-in-law is a nice man but his wife is bad.' And she told me not to say anything because my mother-in-law would throw rocks down on her and try to kill her, so of course I did not say anything. And as soon as my mother-in-law saw me she told me to go get water from the well and collect some wood, so I did but I was so tired and then we sat and everyone talked and I knew that I had to be the last to go to sleep because I am the *nifi*—and one by one they went to sleep but my mother-in-law kept talking and I was so tired. My eyes kept trying to close but I would not let them. But I didn't know—she had this problem that she always fell asleep for a few seconds and then woke up. It happened so fast and it happened many times over the hours that I sat with her but I didn't see her do it. It kept her awake and she never felt tired and finally I couldn't take it and I fell asleep. I couldn't help it!"

Chevi let out a laugh.

"What about the dogs?" someone asked.

She continued, "Well, the next day, I went further up into the mountains with Tomas' sisters to help with the sheep. My father-in-law said to me, 'The sheep dogs will be there. If you are good, you can marry my son, but if you are bad, the dogs will know and they will eat you.' Well, imagine that? I was terrified. I could hear those dogs barking when we were far from the pasture, long before we got to the sheep. They sounded like terrible beasts, much worse than Mitsos' dog!"

She shook her head from side to side with the memory of it.

"As we got to the place with the sheep, they ran toward me with such angry growling faces. I was frozen to the ground. My legs were shaking and my teeth were going like this."

She chattered her teeth together to demonstrate and then continued.

"I almost wet my pants. I was so scared. The dogs growled and barked and surrounded me, showing their teeth and they were pointy and slobbery and I was shaking so hard I could barely stand. But they didn't bite me."

Someone made a joke, "too bad Chevi—you had to marry Tomas!" and the women laughed.

"Chevi, of course, the dogs saw that you were a good woman."

Chevi smiled.

And so the first few hours in the marketplace passed with the chatter of gossip and old stories. And with the morning sun peeking over the mountains, reflecting blue on the returning fishermen in the harbor, Chevi was loading the donkey with empty baskets, her goods all having been sold at a fair price. She returned to her space to help her cousin. And with Chevi's help, Evangelini was next in loading her empty baskets, readying to leave. Her friends from Senitsa, kissing Chevi on both cheeks, wished her well, their next meeting always uncertain. But they, with the other women from the neighboring villages would stay a few more hours, watching the sun grow higher in the sky and when the shadows crept up the post office wall, their products also having been sold, they would be done. It always seemed to be that way.

"Chevi, how is it that you are always first to sell your goods, yet we all have the same?"

Chevi attributed it to the candle she lit every time she passed the church in Agia Kiriaki on her way to market. She did not realize, but the other women guessed, that the soft eyes beneath her black head scarf mesmerized the hearts of the buyers and they were drawn to her like lost children—buying her eggs and snails before they noticed the faces of the other women.

*   *   *   *

In March, little Nikolaos came into the world with a gentle wind whirling within the stone walls of the yard, brushing against the house and causing the empty branches of the pear tree to scratch at the roof tiles of the cooking room in the courtyard below. It had been a particularly rainy month, but on that evening, the moonlight washed over the mountainside

Tomas's young sister, Vaia, had been visiting when the pains began. Yiayia Vasiliki was entertaining the two young women with stories of the village. Tomas had just returned from the village square and had fallen asleep near the fire. Chevi, feeling a rush of warm water soak the seat of her chair and a sudden crush against her pelvis, cried out with a wail that was barely recognizable as human. Panicked, she sank to the floor. This was the thing that killed young women; it had killed her mother and her sister's mother. Yiayia Vasilliki could not stop the fear that spread across her granddaughter's face, but she tried to soothe her.

"Turn onto your back, my child. It's going to be okay." She helped Vaia push the sleeping mat under Chevi.

"Brother! Wake up!" yelled Vaia

She could hardly believe Tomas continued to snore through such commotion. But Tomas only shifted his weight, turning to the side, the breathing of his deep slumber hissing from the corner of his mouth.

"Brother!" Vaia grabbed the poker from the fire.

Tomas was awakened from a splitting pain on the side of his head, his sister's voice breaking through the haze. She stood above him, an iron rod in her hand.

"Go get the midwives!"

Chevi's body convulsed with each cry that pulsed down the mountainside as Tomas took in the scene and ran from the room. Vaia returned to her nifi's side with soothing words of encouragement.

After several hours, Chevi lay damp and exhausted. A screaming baby was brought to her breast. He was beautiful. Raw with pain, she brushed her face lightly in his wisps of white hair. For this, she decided, her marriage was bearable.

*   *   *   *

Days turned to weeks and little Nikos grew fussy. Chevi, exhausted from her daily routine and the addition of a new baby, was overwrought with worry. He seemed to cry most of his waking hours and he awoke at night so often. Wrapped tightly in the sarmanitsa on Chevi's back, as she carried the wood through a ravine, the village echoed with his cries. Sauteria, the priest's wife, called to her. "Chamomile and water, Chevi, with a little sugar. It will soothe his stomach."

The baker's mother heard. "No, no, Coffee grinds and lemon with a drop of water, Chevi. That worked for my Mihali!"

But then Chevi heard talk of the evil eye! She first heard it at the well. Laden with a full wooden barrel and turning to go home, one of the older women pulled her aside and told her.

"Maria had wanted Tomas for her husband; perhaps her jealousy has brought down the evil eye . . . po, po, po terrible thing, poor child."

"What? Maria? Really?" Chevi had no idea. She shook her head slowly. Yes! She remembered. Maria had come close during the church service, admiring her little Nikos, having finally left the house for his forty day blessing.

She ran to Yiayia Vasiliki who knew exactly what to do. The older woman filled a glass with water, poured three drops of olive oil in it, cut a piece of Nikos' fine white hair and sprinkled it into the glass. She whispered the necessary prayers and then pressed it to Nikos' mouth. Confused, the infant opened his round lips looking for the nipple and instead got a spoonful of liquid with hair.

"It's okay now," said Yiayia Vasiliki, as he coughed and sputtered, "he will be fine," but Nikos continued to wail.

The following week, having exhausted all known remedies, Chevi elicited the help of cousin Evangelini to walk with her to see the doctor in Parga. She had a few drachmas left from selling at the market; perhaps it was enough.

They were ushered into the small examination room by the doctor himself.

"Not enough milk," was his diagnosis. The kind doctor refused her last drachmas. "Eat meat and produce more milk," he said. But Chevi had only those few drachmas in her apron pocket. She would not be able to buy any meat. If she killed a chicken, she wouldn't have enough eggs. She and Evangelini discussed what the doctor had said and came up with a solution.

"Thanasi and I will kill a sheep and you will have some mutton to eat." Evangelini knew her husband would agree with such a plan and then they could sell the skin on the next market day to buy some necessary items.

Chevi was satisfied. She did not like to take from her cousin but she knew that she would return the favor when a need arose. So with Nikos securely attached to her back, the two women readied themselves for the trek home. They walked through the center of Parga and passed the butcher's big window as he wielded his cleaver against the giant wooden stump. But that is not where Chevi's eyes were drawn. Instead, she saw, in the jeweler's window, the answer to her son's crying—a little round glass pendant of blue and white with a black dot in the middle. A mati! Yes, of course. She needed to attach that to Nikos' clothing to ward off the evil eye and then she was sure his crying and discomfort would end. She would also take the doctor's advice; after all, he was an educated man. He could read and write like her husband and so, like Tomas, he must know things. But, the mati was sure to work. Anyone from the village would agree as did Evangelini as she followed Chevi's gaze to the jeweler's window. They would come back at the next market day with many eggs and a sheep skin and then they would have enough money to protect poor little Nikos. In the meantime, the mountain trails swallowed the infant's cries as he continued to fuss.

A month passed. Little Nikos grew stronger. Chevi had mutton for as long as it lasted. Finally, she was ready to return to Parga for the mati. She had her eggs and some beans and she knew, with the sheep skin, they would have the money for the jeweler. But she had not realized Evangelini's need for a cooking stove with gas.

"Imagine!" Evangelini said proudly when Chevi arrived at her house, "cooking without wood." She snapped the knob on the white metal box and a blue flame rose.

"Sit, Chevi. Have some coffee." Evangelini began spooning the brown powder into the *brigi*—a tiny long-stemmed copper pot—ready to show off the marvels of the modern world.

Chevi stepped back a few steps, expecting an explosion. She had heard about gas. It was dangerous. What a fool Evangelini was to waste money from the sheep skin on such a contraption. She would still need to collect wood to burn inside the fourno, to cook everything else. And now buying something more useful, like the mati, was out of reach. She was devastated.

Evangelini read her cousin's face. "Chevi, of course you will buy the mati. Nikos is not safe without it." She reached into her apron pocket and brought out some neatly folded drachmas. "Here, I have not forgotten you."

So Nikos got his mati, and the fact that his digestive system was maturing as he grew stronger and the colic that racked his tiny body was subsiding, was not taken into account. It was the mati that cured him. And if there had been someone during my desperate sleepless weeks as a new mother with a colicky first born, who had suggested pinning a piece of round glass to her as a cure, I would have gladly travelled anywhere to get it.

CHAPTER 5

It was the summer of 1987. I was a twenty-eight-year-old mother of two: Nikki, three years old and Thomas, sixteen months. I was lying on a hotel bed that filled a tiny room with an open window that nearly touched the building beside it. It was somewhere after midnight but both lights were on. I was fully clothed, with Nikki face down on my chest, our bodies welded together by the heat that hoarded the breathable air. Little Thomas slept soundly at my side despite the groans of ecstasy that waft in through the open, unscreened window, from a woman in an undefined location.

"She has to be done soon," I thought, but she would continue until daylight.

I gently lifted Nikki to extract her from my body, hoping for some relief, but she looked up at me and shook her head as if to say, "don't even think about it." So I released her to my chest again.

Many hours before, we had said goodbye to Nick at JFK airport, ready to take the night time flight, which in theory meant the passengers could sleep, but was completely unrealistic in the café-like atmosphere among the returning Greeks. We had left Nick behind to work while we hoped to be relaxing in the serenity of the Greek countryside. The plan was that he would join us in a month with my parents. So with two toddlers in tow, I had walked past the security station pushing a cart that was bogged down by the weight of giant boxes of Pampers, a blowup swimming pool, a hammock, numerous suitcases and a mammoth radio—most of which, I would not use. And for so many years we would attempt to mix the two worlds, carting special pie pans and pots for Greek coffee back to New York, nail polish and make-up to the village—never really accepting that it was an undoable task

When we landed in Athens, Vangelis and his wife, Fofo—friends who were originally from the northern area of my destination but had settled in Athens years before—had met us and brought us to their home for the six hour layover, as we waited for our connecting flight to the island of Corfu, where we would then take a ferry to the mainland and finally be driven to Margariti.

With the passing hours, after these friends returned us to the airport and said their goodbyes, I waited in a crowded, un-air-conditioned-smoky room to embark on the next leg of the journey. The departure time came and went. There had been a few announcements, none of which I understood, though someone had attempted to translate them to English. The hours passed. Nikki and Thomas finished the water and cookies I had in my bag. I was such an inexperienced traveller with my naive faith in time and schedules, especially with something as official as an airport. That day would be my first serious lesson in *Greek time*, as I would learn over and over throughout the following years that scheduled times were merely a suggestion and the actual use of time with a clock and its numbers was rare. My question of "when?" was often answered with: *in a few minutes* that really meant hours. The repairman who scheduled his visit for *before lunch* had me wondering, "Is that the two o clock meal before siesta? Should we prepare a place for him at the table, or is he referring to the many hours between waking and *lunchtime*?" And the visitors, who planned to stay for *a few days*, would still be there after a week. *A few, a couple, some.* They were all words with ambiguous meaning, open to the individuals' interpretation. And timetables were there merely as a reference but not to be taken too seriously. This distance between my own New-York-born concept of time and that of the Greeks would continue to plague me for years.

But on that day, we finally boarded the Corfu plane, twenty

hours after leaving New York. As the cabin pressure changed, Thomas pulled at his ears and cried for the entire hour. I was far beyond exhaustion, and I remember thinking that if the engines were to just putter out and we were to go down, I would be okay with that. Really. My judgment and my senses were numb. I was a rag doll with two children pulling at my arms. Landing in Corfu, I saw the full staircase being rolled up to the plane exit and realized that I would have the daunting task of carrying two toddlers, numerous small bags and the giant radio down them. And it appeared by the smell in the air, that Thomas was ready for a diaper change.

That smell, along with my own rankness is what I brought to my two awaiting brother-in-laws, Fotis and Christos. Unfortunately, the delay had caused us to miss the midnight ferry—the last one from Corfu to the mainland, so we drove around in a taxi searching for a hotel. We were lucky to find one with a vacancy and if there hadn't been a monstrously large praying mantis perched on the bed's head board in that room, and if we had seen it before Nikki had—coming out of the shower naked, screaming and running into the hall—our stay there might have provided me with a bit of sleep before the *lady of the night* began her escapades. But, I lay down on that bed, after Fotis and Christos had slain the evil creature, and I was so sleep deprived, I did not have the energy to feel anything. Many years later, Fotis and I would debate about the size of that praying mantis, but I don't think reality has much weight when fear is in control.

So I waited for daybreak—enduring and being the strong adult, with the thought that soon I would have some rest as Margariti lay ahead. Yes, it's true. I longed to be in Margariti.

Hours later, the ferry docked in the bustling port of Igoumenitsa. We were brought to an apartment, embraced by cousins: five-year-old Dina and her younger sister, Marianna. And we were greeted by the aroma of a meal that my sister-in-law, Vaso, had prepared. Unbeknownst to me, we were to stay there for a few days. John, Chevi's father, was dying, laid out in the small two-room house in Margariti, attended to by Chevi and though it was determined by some that the children should not be subjected to that situation and therefore should stay in Igoumenitsa indefinitely, Chevi insisted we be brought to

Margariti, but first she needed a day or two to move her father back to his house up on the mountainside.

So, after having a relaxing shower, bathing the children and spending a pleasant day, I assumed that the reason we were ushered into the bedrooms was because of the late hour, and that the following morning we would, no doubt, be in Margariti.

But the next morning, after some gesturing and pantomime, and a few words of English like, "Go, work, you," Christos and Vaso left the tiny four room apartment, and their children disappeared with them. I was left with my two toddlers—no television, no toys—hours and hours of my keeping them occupied and then silent during siesta time, something their internal clocks knew nothing about. I couldn't understand why I wasn't taken to my destination where the children would be able to run around an endless yard, to play in the dirt, to make as much noise as they needed, and the bus could come and take us to the sea. Why? There were no telephones to connect me to Nick. I felt trapped. Years later, my mother-in-law, Chevi, would describe how she had tried to stay with her daughter to help with her newborns and how she had paced on the tiny balcony, feeling like a prisoner. I supposed this was more a matter of personality than culture, but at that time, several days into my trip, I was having difficulty holding onto my charade of contentment, and I began to unravel. It's not clear to me so many years later, what had propagated it, but I remember just sinking down onto a sofa, the overflow of tears and Christos' panicked call to his wife in the next room, "Vasoooo?"

That is probably how I learned about the Hellenic Telecommunications Organization, or as it was referred to, OTE.

I was brought to a large dark-red official-looking building. There were numerous telephone booths along a wall. Vaso said something to the attendant and then I was ushered into one of them. Did I dial the number or was it done for me? I don't remember, but I do remember the flood of *home* rushing through the receiver and Nick's reassuring voice washing over me. The attendant's gesturing and anxious chatter as he pointed to the rapidly changing numbers being tallied above the phone were dismissed with the wave of Vaso's hand as she stood guard against any intrusion. She could not speak my language, but she seemed to understand this desperate connection.

OTE became one of my favorite places, especially when I found one near the beach in Parga. And I gladly forked over as many drachmas as were necessary to connect me to my life support system in New York. The challenge was in arriving at OTE when it was actually open, as it followed the same limited working hours as all other businesses in Greece and I would be confronted more times by a locked door and a broken heart than by an open one.

CHAPTER 6

The New Year, 1957, approached. Chevi worked at a table close to the fire, pressing hard into the wooden board as she kneaded the dough for the New Year's Bread, the *vasilopita*. Muffled voices could be heard ascending the stairs, hitting the entrance door. It opened with a burst of anger and Nikos watched his *papou*, his grandfather, as the older man entered the room. Tomas stumbled in after him.

"You lazy dog." John spit his words at Tomas. His son-in-law had promised to meet him in the olive grove to prepare for the picking but had been unexpectedly detained at the village taverna. John stomped on the floor, clumps of dried dirt falling from his shoes. Nikos saw the dry dust settle around this grandfather's shoes and then he followed the men to Chevi's work table.

Tomas said something that was not decipherable, ouzo fumes trailing him like a stubborn shadow. He stumbled and knocked the cradle, almost toppling his new daughter. With a heavy sigh, he remembered.

"A girl. Troubles. Worries." He shook his head, and then continued. It was almost a whisper. "But perhaps a strong worker like her mother." He was lost in the reverie of the days ahead, when his children would grow to an age where they could be used for the labor needed. He leaned against the wooden board where Chevi pushed and pulled the dough.

"We need more sons to work in the olive grove." His breath stung her eyes.

Chevi looked from one man to the other. "I need a coin to put in the vasilopita. We cannot have New Year's bread without a coin."

"Put a stone in it," Tomas chuckled, "who will know the difference?" and he walked into the bedroom. The straw mattress whined with his weight.

Chevi looked questioningly at her father. His eyes threw jagged bolts of fire at the bedroom door, but he said nothing and walked out of the house. Chevi, carefully lifted her skirt to reveal her torn and faded undergarment. There was a small pocket with a zipper that had been hand-sewn onto it. She unzipped it and gingerly pulled out a one cent coin. She carefully zipped the pocket again, lowered her dress and kneaded the coin into the bread.

In the morning, Chevi and Yiayia Vasiliki began preparations for the New Year's meal. Evangelini and Thanasi came early with bags of nuts and cinnamon and a chicken that had been plucked and cleaned. Tomas—having anticipated the work needed before the festivities—sat at the taverna with Pavlos, gulping ouzo, his chair resting on the outside of the taverna wall, business closed for the day, for when he had innocently stopped by Markos' house to wish him a Happy New Year, knowing the degree of disgust the taverna owner's wife had for him, the result was as expected. Markos convinced him to walk into town where he would open his taverna for a special holiday cheer. Of course, Pavlos had joined them when he saw the pair pass by, his head entangled in tree branches, retrieving the lemons his wife had requested and at that very moment the sound of her lovely voice bellowing through the open shutter of the kitchen window with a new request. And so he engaged the men in some light conversation, not wanting to be rude, and then walked with them so they were not delayed for whatever business to which they seemed to be hurrying. And after the men raised their glasses to good health and then to prosperity, and once more to abundant harvests, Markos moved the tipsy men to the outer portion of the taverna, generously bringing the rest of the bottle, but locking the other bottles safely within. He then excused himself and returned home to celebrate the New Year with his family. At the same time Chevi, with her grandmother and cousin, was rolling out the wafer thin dough to make pies: spinach pie, sweet milk pie, cheese pie and kolokithi pie with chunks of pumpkin and raisins. They stoked the wood in the fourno until it yielded warm black coals of heat. Then they roasted the chicken, saving some of its meat for avgolemono, a hearty egg and rice soup with the juice of the lemons that little Nikos picked from the bottom branches of the tree when Thanasi pulled the boughs lower, the lemons hanging heavy with their tart juice.

John dragged a long table from the tool shack, placing it under the tree, readying it for the relatives as they began to arrive. The table was one of Tomas' creations, having used scrap pieces of wood and cleverly not wasting too many nails. John found rocks for each leg to steady it so the food would not roll from the table.

Just as the family sat to enjoy the meal, Tomas stumbled up the pathway calling for all to take the sweet *caramellas* he pulled from his pocket. Nikos ran to his father and was rewarded with a fuzzy round candy in his palm. He plucked the dust and loose tobacco from it, examined it carefully, then shrugged his shoulders and popped it in his mouth. It wasn't often that he got to enjoy such a treat; defiled as it was, it was still deliciously sweet.

The men and children took their seats and were served. John cut the vasilopita and passed the chunks of bread around the table. With one bite, Tomas' teeth hit a one cent coin. Plucking it from his mouth he sputtered, "Good luck for me! This year I will have another son!"

But ten months later when his second daughter arrived, he was not discouraged. He assured Chevi he would keep providing her with the seed for more sons, if she would just do her part; she must lie on her right side next time because that is what the men in the taverna had suggested, "and afterwards eat some zucchini with pepper."

"If they are so wise," thought Chevi, "why do they all have daughters?" She rolled her eyes and braced herself. "A fourth child?" She smiled. "Children are a blessing," she thought, "but they need to eat." Now with baby Eftihia on her back, little Vaso at her side, scaling the mountain with water several times a day was back-breaking, even with little Nikos trailing behind with a small water container. Cutting and collecting wood was even more challenging. Thankfully, she had Evangelini and Thanasi to help her, poor dears; they still hadn't had a child.

*   *   *   *

In late March, as Chevi seeded the field with corn, Vaso holding the seed bag, Nikos handing his mother the seeds and Eftihia tethered to a tree in the shade, toddling in the dirt, Tomas discussed some exciting news at the taverna. He had heard something about the government giving away free land. He had his eye on one particular piece, with a house and a farm down near the main road. It was one of the Muslim properties that had been claimed when they had fled. Some people, while living comfortably in a different location, had come and written their names on doors, claiming several different properties. The government had decided to send officials to the countryside to see which buildings were actually inhabited. Those that were not, were confiscated and put in a lottery for those who owned nothing, and since Tomas would not own their family house until John died, Tomas qualified. And since John was still relatively young and quite strong and healthy, Tomas was anxious to get away from him and become the master of his own home. So, he inquired at the Margariti town hall.

Fortunately for Tomas, his buddy Christos, who he often shared a bottle of ouzo with, was the cousin of one of the officials, and brother-in-law of another. When it came time to draw numbers, the number that Tomas drew turned out to be that property he had hoped for. What luck!

Mr. Prasinos in Senitsa, the former owner of that property, was livid. Before it was confiscated from him, he had hoped to build a house for his daughter and her husband from Margariti. She was already twelve years old and had been promised to the son of Mr. Ducas when he finished in the army, but that house had been part of the dowry and was no doubt expected. Mr. Prasinos did not know how he would remedy his situation, but he decided not to tell anyone about the bank loan that existed against the back rooms of that house.

With the news of a new home, Chevi allowed herself to breath in some hope. It had its own private well, it was closer to the main road and there would be much less hauling up the treacherous rocks to her father's house. Also, her childhood friend, Cochina, had moved to Margariti with her husband and children and they were in the process of building a house right across the street from Tomas' new one. To have the company of an old friend would be such a relief from the daily struggle.

On the day of the move, Chevi served her father coffee and then began rolling the thin dough for the last pies she would make in his kitchen. Yiayia Vasiliki had gone to live in Uncle Spyros' house a few years before to help with his three children, but to also be close to that son who she had missed for so many years. But on the day of the move, she was there to help Chevi.

"My son, will you be okay living alone?"

"Yes, of course," he replied, "I cannot stand to live under the same roof as that drunken fool!" He sneered at Tomas, watching him through the open window as he loaded blankets on the back of the donkey in the courtyard. He turned to Chevi, who was absorbed in thoughts of her new home.

"I will be fine here. Chevi, you are nearby so you will bring me my wood and water. Your grandmother is too busy for that now."

Chevi and Yiayia Vasiliki exchanged a look. Both thought about the extra work Chevi would have with two houses and wondered about a possible attempt at finding John a new wife— his fourth.

John had been wondering the same thing. Weeks before, his attention had been pulled to his open gate to admire an unsuspecting, Agapi. She was aptly named, he thought, for her name meant *love* in the Greek language. Her soft yellow curls hung provocatively from her head scarf as she passed his house, her older brother protectively guiding her along the jagged stones. The pair had been passing there every afternoon for years, part of the scenery like the swallows that arched through the air. John only recently noticed her gradual change from a young girl to a woman. But of course, she was out of his reach. The villagers' idle chatter about his lost wives and the rumors born from it—which continued to multiply over the passing years—meant her father would never allow such a union, but it was her image and those tufts of blond hair that propelled him as he and one of his buddies at the taverna discussed several possibilities of matrimony and with each empty glass of ouzo, their ideas became clearer and seemed more reasonable.

"First, you must find a woman of your taste and then steal her from her home, like Yianni the baker's son, did," said Kalofilos. "I have a horse you can use."

What both men failed to realize was that Yianni had been *stealing* his woman from her father who had objected to their marriage, and that she loved Yianni as much as he loved her, and that she had been waiting for him with her possessions packed when he had come to take her. These facts were of no interest to either of them as they continued to plot. Kalofilos absently picked something from his teeth with the broken end of a matchstick, took a sip of ouzo, scratched his beard and looked off into the empty air, deep in thought with his own fantasy.

"Wait a minute, my friend." A problem occurred to John. "How will I ride the horse and tie her up at the same time?"

They discussed several scenarios, each better than the one before and finally the men, believing they had ironed out the chinks in the plan, were ready for action—though it would have benefitted them both to ignore their impulses that night, wait a day, or at least until morning and upon sobering up, they might have seen the obvious lunacy of it all. But instead, Kalofilos staggered home, that being about sixty paces from the taverna and he returned with a rope hanging from his shoulder. John, a bottle of ouzo in one hand, grabbed the back of his friend's neck with his other hand, kissed him on both cheeks and patted him on the back as a reward for his brilliance. Then they set out for Kalofilos' farm to find the horse.

They would have gotten there sooner but the path they took kept bringing them to the wrong farm. Cursing the town grass cutter, for he was the reason the path was awry, they began a long—and sometimes loud—discussion on how to improve the Greek government system, which had allowed such a buffoon to cut the weeds on the path; so inept was he, that they were now being kept from their important task at hand. By then, the moon was high above the mountain peaks, shining a light for them to see a horse tied to a nearby tree, as if Eros, himself, approved of their plan and was leading them to love. John hoisted himself atop the animal. And Kalofilos, tossing him the rope, realized how enormous John was, for his feet were almost touching the ground even though he sat high up on the animal's back.

John raised one hand to catch the rope, the other hand tightly clutching the ouzo bottle, but his attempt at catching it, landed him with a thud on the other side of the *horse*, his back thrown into the dry thistle, his feet stuck up toward the moon and the bottle of ouzo, unhurt, glistening in the night air, held up over his chest by his clenched fist.

"That was some throw, Kalofilos," he said with admiration, as he struggled to his feet, the rope in disarray around his neck and his arms and over one shoulder, hanging and tripping his feet as he tried to steady his wobbling body. The startled animal let out a loud braying sound and in their drunken stupor, they did not notice that the animal John was climbing back up onto, was not actually a horse.

It has been said that the effect of ouzo on the brain distorts one's sense of speed and time, so it is not surprising that John and Kalofilos believed themselves to have been transported with great speed by that proud stallion to the balcony of the beautiful and fair Agapi, whereas in reality, when Tomas, in his new house at the foot of the mountain, looked out over the valley that night as he sat on the make-shift toilet he had fashioned with cinder blocks in his indoor bathroom—a small closet-sized room on the second floor with a wide pipe leading to a ditch far below and an aptly-placed window to control unwanted smells—he saw the silhouette of a slow-moving donkey struggling along a moonlit path with two men on top, swaying up and down and occasionally falling to the ground.

"*Drunken fools,*" he thought as the donkey walked in circles.

John awoke the next afternoon on the floor of his bedroom, near his sleeping mat, with a fuzzy memory of the previous night's events. Most of the villagers in the main square, however, had a clear rendition of those early morning hours and over the years, they kept it alive as it passed from one mouth to another, always with some embellishments as they had been awoken in the early hours of the morning by a commotion outside their windows. John Lykas was singing, *"Agapi mou, Agapi mou,"* which to the Greek villagers meant, *"my love, my love."* Oh, the poor man missed his daughter they thought. He was extremely intoxicated, riding backwards on a donkey, entangled in a long green vine that wrapped around his neck and his arms and over one shoulder.

"Agapi mou, my love, I am here for you!" John had slid from the donkey, falling to the cobbled road, a new bruise added to his war-torn body that suffered from the night's adventure. A sympathetic villager had braced his body against his own, helping him to stand. That man, a father himself of a three year old girl, imagined the pain of losing her when she left his house for marriage.

"It cannot be helped, John. You should be grateful she still lives in the same village," he said gently as he led him through town, passing Kalofilos who was propped up against a tree, eyes closed, a whistling sound coming from his nose and a rooster on his lap, crowing with gusto to alert all in earshot that the sun was on its way. The two continued up the long path to John's house where his neighbor's wife, with a confused furrowing of her brow squinted across the narrow ravine that separated them, to see who was entering his gate so early as she started the morning cooking fire.

News reached Chevi as daylight broke over the mountain ridge. Chavana had been gathering wood from a pile near the front wall of her yard as Mihali passed by on his way to the pasture. He told Chavana how his mother had seen John being led, bruised and battered, through his gate just before dawn. Chavana listened intently and then ran off to share the news with Chevi—and anyone else she passed on her way to Chevi's door.

John had to live with the humiliation of whichever story surfaced. In the clarity of soberness, without the haze of the ouzo—though he would later prefer that haze as life went on—he realized the stupidity of his plan but did not care to discuss it with anyone. Kalofilos seemed to agree.

So it was the matchmaker, who eventually found John his fourth wife. With a few drachmas and a brief description, a single man looking for a wife or a desperate family unable to find a husband for their not-so-desirable bride could usually close a deal. The matchmaker was a married man, himself with two sons and a daughter. One might wonder how such a successful businessman as he, could have failed so miserably with his own daughter some years later when she went off to Athens—a woman alone, unthinkable—and then returned to the village an entrepreneur in a business similar to that of her father's in which she satisfied the needs of her customers, mostly random husbands of the village or an occasional traveler.

Before his thoughts brought him to Antonio, John laid low for a while, embarrassed by his escapade with Kalofilos, and he slowly accepting his limitations as a prospective husband. Then, when the whisper of the lefkes trees started to sound like a woman's voice and when he mistook the singing of a bird for someone calling him to his gate, he decided to visit the matchmaker who then presented John with a possibility. Her name was Vaso, an older person like himself, from behind the mountain, in a village whose name is believed to have been derived from the Greek word for *fairy tale*: Paramithia. It was the place where forty-nine priests and teachers had been executed during the second Great War, the place that always got the rain while the Margaritans watched with thirst as the black clouds emptied into the distance, the place where, four decades later, desperate pleas to European Union officials, paired with a heated competition between officials from neighboring villages, would win its inhabitants the lucrative exit ramp from the Egnatia Highway, built with money from the EU, and lined with Paramithia's gas stations and cafes. But for John, it was a place of real fairy tales because it was the place that brought him his fourth wife, the one he fell in love with: Vaso.

How old was Vaso? It could not definitively be determined, which was not an unusual circumstance, as many of the villagers of that time estimated their ages. Parents often delayed registering their newborns with the town hall for varying reasons. Some bore the child in the fields during harvest and preferred not to interrupt their reaping, others were on the mountains shepherding the sheep, and still others had just forgotten; it was not a priority. The child was alive and appeared healthy. Nothing more was needed. A visit to the registrar could be done on any subsequent trip into town. For many of the older people, most documents would have been destroyed in one of the several wars they endured, so birth dates were often an estimate. Celebrating an added year to one's life was done on the saints' days, so Vaso, short for Vasiliki, the female form of Vasilli, meaning Basil, was celebrated on the first of January every year, Saint Basil's Day. And people estimated that Vaso had celebrated close to the same number as had John, so there it was agreed upon by those in the negotiations of the deal, that the two were *close in age*. But John had no pretenses. He estimated himself to be a man of about fifty eight and his only hope was for someone to soften the deafening silence of the house.

On the day of the wedding, there was an unremarkable ceremony where Father Lou blessed the union. John could not have imagined, and the villagers never guessed, the joy he would have with those next years of marriage. Chevi, her children at her side, came to the church to witness the union and to greet her new mother, the new nifi in town, her children's new grandmother.

John's bride, shrouded in the traditional black dress and black head scarf that was customary of the older women of that time, promised to love, honor and obey and then went home with her new husband to her new home, which had slowly descended into disarray the winter before. John, after having first contemplated collecting wood himself and then having dismissed the idea at the thought of the shame when others might see him doing women's work, had removed the giant wooden gate and disassembled the wooden shed in the yard to keep himself warm when his wood pile had not been replenished quickly enough by Chevi.

Vaso removed her head scarf, her face softened by its removal, revealing a woman who appeared much younger than John had expected. He did not question his luck in getting this younger, attractive woman, nor did he wonder about her apparent commitment to him, her passionate lovemaking, the joy she brought to the home nor the love he felt for her as time pleasantly slipped by. So when the first outbreak of her disfiguring skin disease occurred, he was so thoroughly in love with her, he barely heard the whispers of the villagers around him or noticed how they had stopped inviting them to their houses or knew how, when they left the relatives' homes, their plates and forks were thrown in the garbage and their seats were scrubbed with bleach.

It is hard to be different in a small village, and Margariti was no exception. Vaso's skin ailment was not something that could be hidden. It was there on her face, intermittently under her black shawl, ready to appear without warning or coping mechanisms, by some unfair genetic coding. And so, the villagers turned cool to the new nifi as she became more and more isolated from them and more deeply dedicated to her husband.

Vaso, a woman in her forties, had come from a small village and knew the cruelties that her misunderstood disease brought with it. She was but an innocent child when it first showed itself and it was believed by many to have been a curse put upon someone in the history of the family. Much of its cruelty was in its randomness as her sister and brother would live out normal lives while she was sentenced to a lifetime of misery.

But that was before her union with John. She savored and relished his presence, something no one ever suspected. They saw her only with pity, living as she was in a broken house with an old man who drank too much and offered very little in the way of income. But with John, she had the love and warmth of a man — one whose eyes showed the joy of her presence in a room, who tenderly caressed her blemished body without regard for the purple marks at which others cringed, and above all one who gave her what she longed for, but had resigned herself to a life without. Children.

Chevi welcomed this new mother who was but a decade older than she. They collected wood together and visited the vrisi and Vaso was grateful for that. The nifi's brother from Athens visited John's home occasionally bringing money and gifts. And the shock was felt equally in both families when Vaso's belly began to swell and it was realized that John would become a father again — in his sixties.

Nikos would not remember the wedding or the birth of the first two children, but the baptism of John's and Vaso's third child would stay etched in his mind like the memory of a first kiss. He had been a young boy waiting at the church gates for the baptism to begin so that he could slip away unnoticed. Church events were not his favorite.

The nifi's brother from Athens arrived with his children. Nikos was awestruck by the vision of their 1964 black Mercedes sports coupe, crawling through the donkey-sized streets of the village, a village that, until that moment had seen only a handful of cars. The most memorable was a 1958 Mercedes sedan which had ended up an empty shell on cinderblocks after the owner sold the parts and abandoned it near the preschool, its body transformed into a clubhouse by Nikos and his friends.

But that day, the sports coup approached the village square with the sun reflecting off the windshield, blinding anyone that tried to see within. And Nikos watched, mouth agape, his eleven-year-old eyes wide with wonder as the car rolled to a stop within the walls of the church yard and a young red-headed girl emerged from the back seat, her breasts pushing out of a tight blouse, her hips swiveling inside what much of the world was learning to be a *mini skirt,* and music coming from the open windows of the car, not clarinets or bouzouki, but The Beatles wafting like the scent of juniper into the air.

". . . Ooh, ooh. . . I saw her standing there. . ."

The music stopping abruptly as the car engine cut, and Nikos was changed forever with that slight breeze of the outside world that had blown into the church yard and managed to open the door to the valley ever so slightly.

CHAPTER 7

Why had I left Long Island to spend a summer alone in a foreign country with two small children? I would tell people, that I thought it was important for Nikki and Thomas to see where their father had grown up, and that was true—partially. Our life back in the U.S. was so difficult, the prospect of being alone in a poor remote area of the world where I could not communicate, alone with two small toddlers, one not yet toilet trained, seemed like it might be a refreshing relief from the daily grind of survival back home.

The 1980s in the U.S., according to history, were an era of prosperity. For Nick and me, it was the beginning of a two decade long struggle that would cement our alliance in our fight for a future. At that point I was the wife of a Greek immigrant who was working as a cook in a diner. And as I acquired the knowledge that went with that role, I learned also that without health insurance, the medical profession wanted cash only. The birth of our first child had taken every penny we had saved. But that first hospital bill, with its fifty dollar aspirin and the full day charge for a hospital room that I had checked into only a few minutes before midnight, prompted us, as I went into labor with our second child, to throw some pain reliever into my overnight bag, and then to sit in the parking lot of Smithtown General Hospital, practicing Lamaze-breathing with every contraction until the clock on the dashboard safely passed into the morning of the next billable day. For immunizations we needed cash. Doctor visits: cash. In those days, pharmacies were not the enormous one-stop shopping that they are today, but I could use my credit card there for medication, as well as diapers, shampoo, toothpaste and other toiletries. Using a credit card in a supermarket, though, would not become customary for many more years, so I would put a few food items on the belt, calculating with fingers crossed, asking the cashier for a subtotal after each item.

The debt grew and so did the frustration. I longed to be the television mom of my youth, but I was back at work within weeks after Thomas was born. I worked late nights, waiting on tables, and then dropped into bed not much before Nick was waking to start his twelve hour day, and the children were still too small to sleep past dawn.

Some might have seen futility in our struggle, but they couldn't have known how we came together in stolen moments of plans and promises, supporting each other like the rock-hard cement of the foundation beneath out home. And slowly the delicate tendrils of our dreams began to grow, reaching out to one another through time, sustained by hope, eventually becoming one thick vine moving upward, nourished in the light of the sun.

So knowing the routine that awaited me back home, I approached that summer's adventures with optimism. After the OTE phone call in Igoumenitsa it was determined that we needed to continue on to our destination: Margariti. So we drove in Christos' tiny green car, packed to the brim with Vaso in the front, one child on her lap and I in the backseat with the other three wedged between our belongings. Car seats and seatbelts were not even a remote thought.

The car whined as it bottomed out on the rocks embedded in the dirt of the hill that would eventually be called a driveway, and then it cried to a stop in the courtyard between the main structure and the small house.

Chevi sat with another woman in the shade of the big house at the bottom of the stairs. She put a pan of onions aside and came to the car. The other woman had been spinning a line of shredded sheep's hair onto a small hand-sized piece of round wood — making yarn. She placed it carefully on the steps and followed

Chevi. At the sight of the children, as they piled from the car, the two older women called to them in delight and began kissing, hugging, grabbing, and chattering loudly between themselves and then to Vaso while Christos removed our belongings from the car. And then the other woman grabbed little Thomas.

"Thomooli!" she cried, and before he thought to escape, she had his head in her hands.

"My name's Thomas!" He tried to speak as loudly as he could with his mouth pushed sideways by the hands that sandwiched his face, kisses being planted on his cheeks and forehead, his grimace ignored.

The three little girls, Nikki and her cousins, heard his distress and banned together singing, "Thomooli, Thomooli, Thomooli. . ."

"My name is Thomas!"

It was characteristic of his reaction at times in the U.S. when someone would call him Tom or Tommy assumingly, and he would yell, "My name is Thomas!" which would result in laughter from the adult who had unknowingly threatened to alter his identity. And that is what happened then, in the yard with Chevi and her friend.

Thomooli, meaning little Tomas, is what the villagers would call him until he became taller than his grandfather. But at that time, he never accepted it and would correct anyone who made the error, "My name is Thomas!"

I looked around as I helped empty the car. The area seemed to have fallen into further disarray since my first visit. I wondered about the bathroom since municipal water lines had been connected to each house. Eventually, I would see a haphazardly constructed room with a square in one corner, made from mismatched tiles, the shower head, laying at the end of the snaking hose on the floor which Nick would alter to have coming from the wall, *American-style*, when he arrived the following month. There was a dwarf of a sink and a toilet—a working, flushing toilet. It was all a wonderful sight! And it was on the ground floor. I would still have to walk across the courtyard if I needed it at night, but at least it wasn't up the uneven stairs. The long distant phone calls between Chevi's children had also resulted in a roof on the big house and with it, the memory of the fire faded further. A kitchen was also created next to the bathroom with a working sink, a gas stove and a small refrigerator standing along one wall. All were welcome improvements.

Vaso and Christos spent the day with their children and left the next morning. Nikki and Thomas stayed glued to my side for the first week. We often walked down to the farm with Chevi. The children would feed leaves to the goats and run around with the dog until they were brown with the dry summer dust that settled on everything. We'd go back to the house, wash up and go out for an evening stroll into town. Fotis had acquired a café, so that was usually our destination after a brief stop at the preschool playground which consisted of a small metal push-carousel and some monkey bars. After our evening out, we'd walk back home and sit and look at the starlit sky.

"Look at that moon."

Both children sat on my lap on a wooden chair in the yard, their heads bent upward, resting on my shoulder.

"Let's blow a kiss to it," I'd say as I put a hand to my lips and blew my kiss and they'd do the same as they mimicked me. "That's the same moon that Daddy sees. He'll be looking up at it too and he'll get our kisses and send us back some!"

I missed Nick intensely.

I don't remember how I figured it out, but I eventually realized the bus to Parga made a stop around ten in the morning every weekday out on the main road. So one day, we went and stood at the spot where Nick and I had been dropped off a few years before. Sure enough, people began to gather on the opposite side and seeing our beach garb, they beckoned to us, so we crossed the hot asphalt and waited with them. The bus came. I was able to read the destination in Greek letters. Parga. The ticket writer would not take my money. He handed me the tickets and pointed to an older couple at the back of the bus. Chevi's neighbors, Cochos and Cochina were there with three of their grandsons. I understood their smiles. I waved and smiled back at them and when the bus stopped on the corner near the high school on the outskirts of Parga, we disembarked and I followed them, my two children hand-in-hand beside me, to the beach named *Piso-Krioneri* which means *behind-cold-water*, but I had wanted to go to the heart of town where the main beach was, but I was too unsure. I gladly accepted their coaxing gestures, following them like a duckling to the water and we would be beach companions for most of that month.

Nikki was very wary of the water and wanted to sit on the towel or walk in up to her knees, but Thomas jumped in and splashed, laughing and screaming. He wanted to go out further but Nikki's protests stopped us.

After a few hours, Cochina would begin collecting the towels, yelling to her grandchildren. We'd walk to a café, the same one everyday, where Cochos would talk with the proprietor who would bring us into the kitchen and show us what had been cooked that day, and after much conversing between them and with his wife and his grandchildren, food would be ordered.

"I'm starved!" Nikki would say or Thomas would point, "I want that," as we passed a table with food.

I had mistakenly believed Cochos to be an old villager with limited funds and could not bare to be a burden on him—but my children were hungry. I would wave off his frequent and fervent offers as he pushed plates of fried potatoes, chicken, colorful salads toward me, eyeing me with frustration as I picked at the food insuring that what had been ordered would satisfy all the little ones. I didn't understand the importance of accepting his offer of food, the underlying offer of friendship, but also the grave responsibility that he felt, that he was unable to express to me:

"Your mother-in-law is our neighbor. Our friend. A kind of *family member*. We know the stress you feel in a place you cannot speak. You are young. Your children need food. Let us care for you."

The green beans, the okra, the garlic and yogurt sauce all tried to convey that message but to no avail, as my children and the others at the table fed their ravenous appetites. I would learn later that Cochos had worked many years in Germany, had brought his Greek-speaking wife and children there for a time, but during that summer he was enjoying retirement and the fruits of that labor with a generous pension that converted drachmas into a restful life on the Greek countryside.

But, those excursions did teach me the process for getting food in those old-time cafes and after a while, I found my courage and ventured away from Margariti alone with the children, spending every day in Parga—swimming, eating, hiking up the steep stairs to the castle and back, napping in the cool shade until the evening bus dropped us, toasted and salty back at the Margariti roadside.

One morning, Nikki decided she had had enough of the beach.

"I don't wanna go!" She stood with her hands on her hips, "I wanna stay with my yiayia."

Her yiayia was Chevi and I knew that Chevi was still attending to her dying father.

"C'mon, Nikki, we'll come back on the earlier bus." I was shoving beach towels into a large black canvas bag that was set on the table under the grape arbor.

"No, I'm staying," her lips folded into a pout.

Well, I certainly did not want to drag a crying child to the bus stop.

Chevi rounded the corner of the house with a basket of wet laundry. She listened and watched as she began hanging the damp clothes with pins on the line.

She sensed the conversation between us and walked over to where we were standing. With much gesturing and a few Greek words and phrases, we arranged to have Nikki stay with her while Thomas and I went to Parga. I brought Nikki into the house and showed her the clock.

"When the little hand is on the two, we'll be back." I worried that she would change her mind once we had left, but she seemed unfazed.

I spent an uneasy day at the beach with Thomas and came home on the first bus, eager to see my little girl. As it turned out, she felt the lucky one, having remained in Margariti.

"I goed up a mountain and yiayia gived me cookies and I helped papou Tomas clean my shoes," she proclaimed with the breathless joy only a child can produce.

Actually, she had accompanied Chevi on the steep trail to her father's house and had been distracted with a box of cookies while Chevi tended to her father. Then, on the way back, she had run onto the newly tarred road and had gotten clumps of black goo all over her sneakers. In her three-year-old mind, she had been on an exciting adventure.

Soon after that, there must have been a funeral because I know that John died that summer, but I do not recall seeing or hearing anything that indicated it. I'm sure Chevi and her daughters went to great lengths to keep that information from us.

I learned so much Greek in that month before Nick arrived. I was so lonely for adult company, if someone invited me into the yard as I walked past, I'd accept. Mostly, I just sat and nodded my head in agreement to whatever was said, "uhuh, oh yes" and they would talk and talk and I would smile without understanding a word, but I felt energized by the boldness of it.

But then Cochina came from across the street and took me to her house for coffee. I froze as I entered her doorway. Stunned. And then slowly I proceeded, looking around at the beautifully tiled floors, polished wooden ceilings, modern kitchen with: counters, cabinets, appliances, even a dishwasher! The lace curtains caught in the breeze and blew inward as we sat on her sofa and looked at family photo albums. She served us sweets on glass plates that looked like crystal. When I left that house, I was completely downtrodden. With a heavy sigh, I realized that I had not—in those two visits to Greece—been experiencing authentic rural life, but rather one family's misery. As I walked back to the house, I began to understand Chevi's reason for the animals, her daily escape from the squalor as she stopped to visit with friends on her way . . . and then I secretly hoped that she had found some kind of love on those walks down to the farm. As I climbed the driveway, and the disarray came into view, I began to see Margariti life through different eyes.

A few weeks later we met Nick and my parents at the Igoumenitsa port. Through Fotis, we had reserved a hotel room in Parga for my parents as I wasn't sure they would be ready for the shock of the family house.

That night, I melted into Nick's arms, inhaling deeply, feeling myself strengthen. After that, no one looked my way. Information was passed through him like a strainer. In the rare occasion where someone tried to speak to me, the gears that brought their words inward to be meshed with the English in my brain, appeared to grind too slowly, as the speaker would look toward Nick for his answer before I was able to pull the words out in my broken Greek. I felt it a small price to pay, to have the company of someone I could converse with.

My parents took a side-trip to Italy to visit my father's relatives and they returned in time for Thomas' baptism at the local church.

*   *   *   *

Under the brightly painted icons, I moved toward my small son as I caught his wide eyes fixed on mine.

"Mommy!" Thomas screamed as his fourteen-year-old Godfather, Akis, tried to disrobe him but in the panic, arms and legs became entangled in sleeves and pant legs.

"Mommy!"

"It's okay; Akis won't hurt you," I said as I reached for him.

I helped Akis gently lift my son from his mangled clothing. Thomas liked his adolescent Godfather very much, as he was someone who always seemed to have time for fun, but that unwelcome new activity was now creating a scowl of distrust on Thomas' face.

"No! go out." His little finger pointed to the church door, but he was quickly whisked away and was being carried up to the caldron of holy water near the altar, his cries escalating, "mommy!"

I kept one hand on his warm back as I tried to keep pace with the others.

"I'm here honey . . . I'm here."

"Hey! What are you doing to my brother!?" Nikki grabbed at the priest's robes as he took the screaming little boy in his arms. She was ready to execute some kind of rescue as she pulled back her leg for a kick, but Nick scooped her into his arms. And I wondered at the wisdom of subjecting small children to such a ritual.

The relatives stood about with wide smiles, talking and pointing at Nikki as she continued her efforts.

"Hey!" From Nick's arms she lunged forward to grab for the priest as he submerged Thomas up to his chest, and then she looked at me in wonder. "Mom!?"

"It's okay . . . okay." I held her hand. Her anger remained.

There were prayers and chanting between loud angry protests from Thomas. Water laced with olive oil was poured on his head. He sputtered and continued his cries. More praying, more oil, more water and after an eternity passed, it was over. He grabbed for me and I enveloped him in my arms, wrapped in a towel.

"It's okay, it's okay." I whispered, my lips brushing his face lightly, "shhh, okay now," and he was quiet.

The celebration was only a few steps from the church in Fotis' café. The adults ate and drank and talked; I had my parents to talk to. The children ran around the giant tree near the café and played in the dirt beneath it, laughing and enjoying the common language of play.

*   *   *   *

The following summer arrived with an empty bank account and the realization that there would be no Margariti-distraction from our daily grind in the U.S. We continued our grueling work routine, leaving our children in the care of family members on weekends, evenings, and holidays—all times that I ached to be with them—while we worked the back-breaking hours that were required. Nick and I talked often of alternative plans, searching for an answer. It was decided that he would find time in the evenings to go to school. He was much more knowledgeable than I about most subjects, so after his twelve hour shift in the diner, my parents watched the children as he went off to night school to get his GED—a high school diploma. He was frustrated by the language, and the instructor recommended something called ESL—but that would take so much longer. After much discussion and some gentle pushing from my youngest sister, Joanne, I decided that I would enroll in the local community college.

At that time, Joanne was enrolled in a university, on her way to a Bachelor's degree. To the discomfort of my father, she had left her job at Grumman Aerospace, one he had taken great trouble to secure for her. As it happened, my parents, like many others of that time, saw the wisdom in encouraging their sons to further their education but did not see the reason to waste a girl's time when her final destination was marriage. They did not have the foresight to realize that if marriage had been their only goal for their three daughters, then college would have provided a well-stocked dating pool. But soon after Joanne started the job in Grumman's personnel department, she was given a task that required her to enter employee salaries into a file. As she looked over the data, she suddenly realized that those with a college education were paid twice that of those without. That was the first secret she uncovered. The second one, which she tried to convey to me after completing her first semester, was that there were an awful lot of dummies at college and the "*you're not college material*" that we had grown up with, did not seem to hold water. But I was in no way convinced. I had already walked down that road and seen for myself that I wasn't smart enough to cut it.

Several years before, having left home to free myself from, what seemed to me to be oppressive parental rules, and to find my own space away from my younger siblings, I had moved to a basement apartment one town over and was waitressing in a diner. My brother, Jim, had convinced me to go to the community college by paying for it and persuasively suggesting that he was making a great living as a computer programmer and so could I. So I enrolled in Accounting Class and Cobalt Computer Language in the evenings. I played with the idea of taking an English class but then rejected it as others had told me that English would be too difficult. It had lots of reading and writing and talking about literature which sounded fascinating to me, but I knew I couldn't trust my judgment; I just wasn't smart enough. It turned out that I was right in that regard: I hated both classes and I squeaked by with a mediocre grade and then didn't go back. I wasn't college material.

But a few years later, with Joanne's convincing, I thought that maybe a college course—just one . . . with no math or computers—could be an escape from the drudge that was pulling heavily at my psyche and possibly it might make waiting on tables bearable. So that summer I enrolled in Freshman English at Suffolk Community College which meant that Nick would have to work one more day, a full seven to pay for the class and make up for my decreased working hours.

At the end of six weeks, I stood in the kitchen of the apartment that my parents had added onto their home and I held my grade report for that semester.

"Oh no," I looked at the rectangular paper and slowly ripped each perforated edge until it was open.

"This is it," I whispered. Only Thomas was in the room, playing with toys on the tiled floor. He looked up when he heard me speak.

I slowly pulled the paper apart.

My scream startled him.

It was an A.

I picked him off the floor and threw him into the air. The ceiling fan almost clipped his head as he squealed in delight.

"An A . . . an A!"

One tiny printed letter — a work of art. I couldn't stop looking at it.

I whispered to no one, "A," and my lips curled to a smile. I giggled.

"An A."

I was hooked. I wanted more of those.

So, I would continue on, working at night and going to school during the day as Nikki started kindergarten that autumn and Thomas came with me to the day care center on campus. I was the older woman in the class, ruining the grading curve. I was obsessed with being *college material* and eventually, I would go on to graduate cum laude with a Bachelors of Arts in English and then finish up with a Masters of Arts in the Speech and Hearing Sciences. In the end I would have certification and licensure for teaching secondary English, teaching English as a Second Language (ESL), teaching the speech and hearing disabled, and working as a speech pathologist.

In those early days though, I would wake up at three in the morning to do my school work, then get Nikki and Thomas off to school before driving to my classes, and then home again before the afternoon school bus came. Then I was off to the restaurant to pick up dollars off tables. It was grueling but the alternative was worse. And I remember the wife of one of the restaurant owner's saying to me, as I waited on her and her mother, *"I could never do what you are doing; it'd be too unfair to my children,"* her words scraping deeply at an open wound that would never heal.

But Nick remembered what he had been told long ago by the father of his friend, Vangelis.

"Someone has to lie down in the dirt, in order for the others to rise."

It had been in response to a question Nick had asked about the success of that man's children when all around seemed so poor.

So that year, Nick lay down, face first in the muck as I began my slow ten-year walk unsteadily across his back. At times I had to hold my arms out for balance as he rocked back and forth, in danger of drowning in the shit that was thrown at him, but he simply opened his mouth to swallow it and then settled into stillness, in an effort to make my trip smoother.

CHAPTER 8

In 1963, John's new wife gave him his only son, Chevi's half-brother, Costas. He would be the only one of John's three children with Vaso to suffer from the skin disease—sentencing him to a lonely life in the village. The ouzo with which he medicated that loneliness would bring his life to an end forty six years later. But at that time, the status quo continued in Margariti. The men, the women, and the children all had roles well defined.

Several months before Costas' birth, one day in the beginning of autumn, Chevi's life and the lives of her children were once more dictated by the incompetence of those with power.

Intense heat seared through Anastasia's skin. Escape was impossible. Her screams—the only tool she had to alert them—grew louder, but no one came to her rescue. It was burning the side of her face, melting her skin, making her head feel like the charred wood coals of the fourno which she did not yet know existed, but—because she was not a son—would soon become acquainted with, as she grew and learned to be a good wife. But then, she was only a small infant trapped in a cradle with narrow wooden sides. It had been place, earlier in the day, next to an empty unlit fireplace. Earlier, she had gurgled happily, waving her hands, watching the children play around her—unaware—as the fireplace walls became alit with burning twigs. But when the flames grew, and the heat rose and blazed within the fireplace, she became desperate for relief from the hurt that seemed to singe every nerve in her body. She was the newest addition to the family, baby Anastasia, waiting for rescue—her wailing unheeded, the pain, the heat, the side of her head throbbing.

Nikos and little Vaso were fascinated by the flame and might have been too young to understand its danger as it licked the outside of the fireplace wall, up past the mantle. In fact, they were fascinated by the result of each new piece of wood they threw in, maybe even a little competitive, seeing who could carry the heavier piece, who could throw from the furthest distance in the room as sparks burst in all directions.

From his yard across the dirt path, Miti heard the cracking wood beams and popping roof tiles, as flames shot through the top of his cousin's house. He would never remember how he got to her front yard, or how he took two steps at a time, scaling the stairs to the entrance of the house on the second floor, shouting.

"Get out! Get out! Fire! Chevi! Tomas!"

Nikos and Vaso were sufficiently startled by the urgency in his voice, and they ran for the door and past him, as his hulking body filled the space. At the bottom step, Nikos looked up and saw the red tiles falling into themselves, the roof collapsing as Miti, his face gray with smears of smoke, appeared again, struggling through the door frame with a cradle in his outstretched arms. Behind him the sound of tiles falling to the dirt inside the house and on top of one another—breaking like glass—mixed with baby Anastasia's cries.

Smoke in the village was not uncommon, as it was the tool for cooking everything and for disposing of any garbage that the chickens and goats would not eat, so no one paid attention until the cloud became larger and blacker than usual. Then slowly, people began to sense something different—an odor in that particular mountain smoke that made them stop, sniff, turn their heads.

Chevi, was on her way home from Parga, her market profits tucked tightly in the hidden pocket of her under garment. Little Eftihia toddled next to her, as they crested the dirt path at the top of Senitsa with the expectation of a short visit to gossip with some friends before heading home, but instead, Chevi saw the smoke in the distance across the valley. The barren landscape showed her a gray cloud rising from somewhere near her house. Fraught with worry for her neighbors, she scooped Eftihia onto her back and continued on toward home.

"Did Cochina's husband try to burn those branches?" She remembered that he had been pruning his fruit trees the day before, but he usually tossed them into a pile to be burned later in the rainy season. To burn anything then, at that dry rainless time, she knew would be risky. And Cochos was a responsible person. He took care of his family and worked hard to feed them.

"No," she thought, *"it must be something else."*

She was in a hurry but she was also anxious to see that the beans had been picked, and she was just passing by the farm. She knew how the children might be slowing down Tomas' work. But the beans had not been picked at all and Tomas was nowhere to be seen. Her heart began to race; uneasiness swallowed her and she continued toward home.

What she did not realize, however, was that Tomas had been *called* to the cafenio for something of great importance, shortly after she had left for Parga that morning. He had planned to stay for one small drink and be away for only a short time. But when he got to the cafenio, Pavlos had called him to his table, and as he sat there he heard talk of the possible issuing of a new coin—a thirty drachma coin, commemorating something about which he wasn't quite sure, but Tomas felt—as did many other men in the village—it warranted a deeper discussion over a glass of ouzo . . . or several. Now, sometimes when such discussions got a little intense, or if more participants arrived during the heat of it, one could lose track of time. It could happen to any man, at any time—getting lost in the plethora of ideas in such a consortium as this one had been. And though it is not well known, but it is absolutely true, even Plato—the great philosopher—used to get so wrapped up in his discussions about caves and shadows, that he could spend days at a time, in any given taverna until his wife would come and pull him home by the ear, reminding him that the crops had to be harvested. So, Tomas was with the best of them, when faulted for losing track of time, in a hot discussion at a cafenio, and that is where he was when Miti's father found him.

Chevi, trotted up the hill to the house with Eftihia holding her neck, bouncing with each step. The fact that it was *her* house burning, was not yet fully realized, as Chevi was not completely registering the scene her eyes were taking in, still clinging to the hope that Tomas was with Nikos and Vaso, if not at the farm, then somewhere else and that baby Anastasia was with Cochina, as Chevi had suggested before leaving that morning. Finding the beans unpicked, moments before, had not produced a sense of alarm but rather something more like frustration. And when she had turned toward home, there was that uneasy feeling, born among the bean plants and growing as she hurried along the familiar rocky path, a feeling that she did not examine but felt stirring in her stomach and rising into her throat, pulling at the knowledge of having—for her husband, her master, her legal guardian—a man who never wavered in his incompetence, always producing very little that was useful to the family and much disappointment. But those thoughts simmered below the waters of her consciousness; she would not allow them to surface, as it happens sometimes when the need to survive surpasses the desire to examine that which cannot be changed.

She saw Cochina, the air thick with billowing smoke as she ran toward Chevi clutching a bundle—a baby—and briefly in the periphery of her vision there were Nikos and little Vaso, half hidden behind her cousin Miti and she knew her attention needed to be on this bundle that was coming closer, then thrust into her arms. The weight of Eftihia disappeared, and she saw Anastasia, her baby, the side of her face oozing and then she heard the cries and then the voices.

"Chavos! Chevi, we need Chavos!" And she turned to run to town, to find the person who could fix the screaming child. The healer, Chavos Bakis. He had ointments and herbs and he knew about the stars and the spirits. Chevi, with her baby pulled to her breast—ran. The child's skin smearing on her bodice. She was acutely aware of people running with her, people joining the moving group as they passed villagers questioning the commotion. She ran past the preschool, past the mill, up the steep incline of the cobbled main street, some blurred vision of Tomas among the faces, Pavlos pushing him forward.

Chavos Bakis rushed to meet Chevi. The news of the burned child, as with all village news, had its own speed—like the flash of light before a rumble of thunder—and it preceded the mother and child as they reached him. So Chavos grabbed tiny Anastasia and began his work even before he got to the entrance of his shop. He pushed through the crowd that had closed around him. With Chevi at his side, Tomas being swept to them by hidden hands, the three adults entered the dark room, closing the crowd behind them.

As Chavos attempted to alleviate the child's pain with a sticky ointment of mysterious leaves soaked to softness in olive oil, Chevi soothed her child with cooing sounds and a smooth touch to her arms and legs. And Tomas, as he slowly sobered, met his wife's accusing eyes with a gaze dripping in guilt. The fact remained however—and he was reassuring himself of that very fact at that moment—that he was the master of that family. He was the one who by nature of his sex, owned the house and had custody of the children, including that one whimpering in the arms of the healer. And if he, as the master of the family, had chosen to attend to business of whatever nature he saw fit, before going to the farm that morning, then that was the priority of the day. He had left Nikos and Vaso to watch the child. They were the culprits in this. They were irresponsible, especially Nikos, the man of the house when his father was not present and he would teach him to guard that responsibility. Tomas was thinking of the stick he would use for the beating—one that any parent would condone because, after all, children must be taught to be responsible— when Chevi broke his thoughts.

"Tomas, we need to take her to the doctor in Parga."

But to take her to the doctor, to take her anywhere but back home to the roofless stones, would be to invite the accusing looks of his neighbors, to admit the need for a cure to this mishap that had befallen her on his watch, when none was needed. The healer had done his job and now he would take his family home, to *his* house. Niko would answer for this and it would be done.

"No doctor," said Tomas without explanation.

Chevi did not understand his response but knew she was powerless to change it.

*   *   *   *

The house, an empty stone structure that looked like the remnants of a bomb blast, stood with its tall walls—two stories high—and large windows staring blankly out from a spiritless shell. It still contained one small room with a sagging roof, somehow spared by the fire. The family's meager possessions—sheepskin blankets, a black pot for soup, two round pans for pies, the dishes that Chevi had taken from her father's house, the wooden chest containing seasonal clothes and random kitchen utensils that she had started collecting in anticipation of her future nifi—were all piled along the walls of that room. And that is the room where the family would sleep on the two beds that were in the house when they moved there, large creaking metal frames with thin foam mattresses sagging with the memory of their former occupants. Tomas slept in one bed alone, for he needed as much undisturbed sleep as possible. Chevi slept in the only other bed with Anastasia and Eftihia snuggled against her while Nikos and Vaso slept on mats between the beds which they preferred, especially when an infestation of bedbugs sent the others into a frenzy and Chevi had to drag the mattresses outside and pour boiling water on the foam pads. The small black bugs would drain off and then the heavy water-laden foam would be put out to dry. For the sleeping mats, if needed, new reeds were collected from the swamp, stripped of their leaves and weaved tightly together.

So this was the room the family inhabited until Chevi realized she was going to have another child, her fifth. By this time, Nikos and Vaso were old enough to help their father pile cinderblocks to make two small rooms at the foot of the stairs outside. But the expanding family brought renewed worries to Chevi—one more mouth to feed.

CHAPTER 9

It was the summer of 1991. I was a thirty-two-year-old nifi, again in Margariti looking for some peace behind a closed door. The water from the shower head splashed down onto the tiny sink and like a downpour on a tin roof, heavy drops pulsed from my elbows onto a small washing machine in the corner. But I could still hear the commotion on the other side of the wall, and then knocking that turned to pounding accompanied by a frenzy of other sounds thrown against the bathroom door.

"What?!" Shampoo dripping in my eyes, I turned off the water.

"Aunt Joanne is here! She's here!" I knew Thomas was jumping up and down by the sound of his words as they met my ear.

"Okay, okay, tell her I'll be right out . . . Joanne?" I peeked around the half opened door.

"No mommy. She's in town. Uncle Fotis just came and told us."

Nikki must have been standing there, but I only remember Thomas and that may be because I had often, afterwards, heard my sister's version of her first moments in Margariti.

Back in New York, as summer had approached, it had been clear that there would once again be no funds for a trip to Greece but I could not bear the idea of those endless days of creating activities for a kindergartener and second-grader, within the fog of exhaustion, Nick and I seeing each other only if he happened to wake up as I slid into bed after my night of carrying heavy trays and bouncing between the discontent of cooks and customers. So, we decided that if we were going to be kept apart and in a perpetual state of fatigue, at least I could do it from Greece where the drachma could be stretched to great lengths and the children could spend time immersed in their other culture. But Nick would have to stay back on Long Island, working in the sweltering summer kitchen for his usual seven-day work week.

Joanne had just graduated and had decided to come with us, delaying a job search. We would spend a few days together in Athens at Vangelis and Fofo's house and then she would travel the islands with their daughter while I would head to Margariti with the children.

So there I was, my soapy head sticking out of the open bathroom door. I heard Fotis' motorcycle descending the driveway and wondered why he hadn't just brought Joanne on the back of it — probably a language issue.

Joanne was waiting patiently at his café, the taxi from Athens having deposited her there after an eight hour ride that she'd shared with three other strangers, her head pressed against the back door window eager to finally see our familiar faces after two weeks.

As she sat there at his café, Fotis returned, set his motorcycle on its kickstand, smiled, and went inside.

"What the . . ." Joanne waited . . . and waited, a lump forming in her throat, fighting tears and then she saw a little bronze boy — sun-bleached-white hair and freckled — come running toward her, barefooted on the gravel road.

"Thomas?"

He came closer and wrapped his arms around her waist as she got to her feet and they almost tumbled backwards.

"*This must be a safe place,*" she thought, "*if she let him come alone,*" but to him, she said, "Where's mommy?"

"Shower." He disappeared into the café and returned with an orange soda.

"Huh? Where'd you get that?"

"Uncle Fotis." He jumped up onto a chair and sat with his feet dangling, giddy with the joy of having *his* Aunt Joanne there in that place all to himself.

"Is mommy coming?" Joanne was perplexed at seeing this small child there alone, the same child whose mother — her sister — would not allow in the front yard alone.

"She's taking a shower." He swung his legs back and forth as they hung from the edge of the chair.

Joanne, with a furrowed brow, looked from the small child to Fotis behind the bar, within his café. He met her eyes, nodded and smiled.

"Thomas, where's the house? Can you show me?"

"Well," he emptied the bottle with one last gulp, "will you give me a piggy-back ride?"

"Yes! Get up. Let's go." She helped him onto her back – with the expectation that it would be just around the corner, because after all, this small child had come alone!

She picked up her bag and walked across the plaza. The villagers then understood that the stranger who had been dropped there by a taxi, was *one of their own*, seeing Tomas' grandson with her, and they smiled and nodded as the pair passed by — past the mill, past the preschool and the vrisi and around the bend.

"Where's the house, Thomas?" Beads of perspiration dripped into her eyes as she breathed heavily.

"Just keep going that way." He pointed straight ahead. The bag in her hand grew heavier as she continued to walk.

Joanne once told me that she thought I had spent most of my life blow-drying my hair. She remembered always seeing me — her teenaged sister — in the little downstairs bathroom at home, the hair dryer humming away as I pulled and tugged, trying to tame the wild mane. That day, as she huffed up the driveway, Thomas on her back, his encrusted feet scraping at her side and kicking at the suitcase, she found me in the little house — blow-drying my hair.

"Linda?!" The tears began to well. "How could you leave me there?" And then a flood. "You're blow-drying your hair?" She dropped Thomas, and Nikki appeared from somewhere and they both looked up at her with distress in their eyes, and then they looked at me for guidance.

I pulled her into my arms.

"I'm so sorry. . ."

And both children drew close, hugging our legs, encircling their aunt until she was still. I couldn't explain to her, and she wouldn't have understood, my insecurity at having the villagers see me, Nick's wife, Chevi's nifi, less than perfectly groomed and well-coiffed, that I was a moving target whenever I went into town—eyes from every corner following me—and I was afraid to be seen as the flawed person I actually was. And as we four stood together, encased as one, I was not aware of when my transformation had begun, or how I had forgotten those feelings of strangeness I had felt on my first visit to Margariti as was occurring for Joanne then. And how I was slowly becoming part of that place, but it was not yet a conscious thought.

The four of us spent a week enjoying the sea and sharing stories of our adventures. Joanne told us of her travels to the islands of Santorini and Mykonos, beautiful places to which she hoped to someday return. She talked about the difficulty of travelling with someone who does not share your language, a lonely situation that I understood, and the relief of getting into the taxi to be reunited in our small northern village—an unspoken realization that simple pleasure is derived from the people around us rather than the glamour of an environment.

I told Joanne of one particular story that tickled us all. It was the day Chevi decided to go with me and the children to the beach.

I had known enough Greek to understand that she was telling us that she would join us that day, though I was perplexed at the reason for that sudden change in her character. Perhaps, she felt obligated because Chochina and Cochos had accompanied us at times during our previous trip to Greece. Or maybe she felt that her son would appreciate that extra effort his mother was making for her nifi and grandchildren. In any event, it created an anxiety in me as I feared that she would die there—on Parga Beach—for I watched her descend the bus stairs in her long black dress, black apron and black head scarf. The absence of her black stockings was the only indication that she was wearing beach attire. As we approached the waterfront, she began wiping her brow with the ends of the head scarf, smiling, following us onto the beach, her shoes filling with sand. I laid the towels out. I had no umbrella. There was no money for such luxuries and I had never needed one as we three always spent most of the time in the water and then we would move to a café or other shaded location. But on that day, I wasn't really sure how to proceed. Thomas, as usual was eager to get in the water.

We played in the shallow water for a while, but I didn't know what to do with my mother-in-law. She sat on the towel, smiling, her legs stretched out in front of her, occasionally responding to the Greek questions thrown her way by onlookers who were undoubtedly assessing the odd group before them: one village woman covered in black, two bleached blond children speaking what many people mistook as German, and me—a younger obviously foreign woman with dark hair, who might have been the children's mother, in a bikini.

"Nikki, you stay here with yiayia," I smiled as I knew Chevi would only understand the word *yiayia*.

"Oh mom . . ."

Thomas enjoyed what felt to him like favoritism. "Let's swim to the island, mom!" He sang as he danced back and forth on the sand. The island was a few hundred meters in front of us. It had a little church on it and it was a favorite place for swimmers to go.

Nikki started to whine, "Oh, no . . . I wanna go too!"

Still smiling, I implored, "I'll take you tomorrow. I promise."

I heard her sigh as we swam away.

As we returned a bit later, I saw both my daughter and my mother-in-law in the water. Chevi had gathered her dress around her thighs and was wading up to her knees. Two fishermen stood together on a nearby boat watching the older woman.

"She is going to die from heat exhaustion," I thought, *"and it's going to be my fault. I have to get her out of here."*

As we all dried off, I took Nikki's small straw hat and handed it to Chevi who once again was sitting on the towel with outstretched legs. She took it and put it on top of her head scarf and it sat there like a small clown hat.

We shortened that beach visit considerably that day and were back in Margariti by mid-afternoon. Chevi would tell people that I was embarrassed by the bare-breasted women sunbathing around us and I had rushed her off the beach so she would not see them. But when I described my version of that scene to Joanne as we sat with Nikki and Thomas on a bed in the little house, we all laughed and the kids rolled around on the bunched up sheets — enjoying the comfort of the laughter.

Before Joanne's visit, Nick's sisters and their children had been coming to the village every weekend, as well as having us stay with them on occasion. The children all stuck to me like magnets. There were five of them, close in age, including Nikki and Thomas. They saw that I was not a real participant in that impregnable world of adults and thus I appeared to rarely be occupied, so they hung on me and if I were out of reach, they called to me, "Aunt, look here." I knew that Greek phrase well. And that was how my visit was going on one of the days we had been brought to Igoumenitsa — the day I met the Australian.

I shared this story with Joanne, one evening when she and I went into town to enjoy some Margariti night life, free of the brood. We sat and shared a bottle of wine and discussed our Greek experiences. We were the only women at the café — scandal averted by the fact that it was my brother-in-law's café, we were both foreigners, and we sat quietly away from the others, deeply immersed in our own conversation.

I began my story: The reason I had been with Nikki and Thomas in Igoumenitsa had been for some kind of celebration at the apartment of Christos and Vaso — a name day, a birthday, a national holiday — I don't remember. But the children had been allowed to go around the corner with an older niece of Christos' to visit his elderly mother. About an hour later, I was sitting on a sofa, the words in the crowded room flying by my ears, some of them understandable, yet without any clear meaning, and the five children filed noisily back into the apartment, breathless and wet with sweat. Nikki came to me with red eyes.

"Mommy, they brought me to a witch's house."

Thomas stood behind her, unperturbed, chocolate smeared from ear to ear.

Nikki continued, "I wanted to come back, but they closed the door."

Marianna came near us. "Nikki," she sang her cousin's name. "It's okay, it's okay." She and her sister had picked up some English phrases while listening to their American cousins. *It's okay*, was the most common, followed by a close second phrase: *shut up, stupid*, which hit me with a rush of shame when I heard it in their sweet little Greek accents but I couldn't seem to discourage it as Nikki and Thomas would giggle uncontrollably and the girls would enjoy the feedback.

Again, Marianna cooed. "It's okay, Nikki. It's okay."

"Mommy, I tried to leave." She put her arm around my neck and sniffled, "but they kept giving me candy. I wanted to go, so I had to cry and then they let me out."

Just then, the elderly woman made her way into the apartment with the help of the older niece.

Nikki cowered. "There's the witch!"

From across the room, a young woman laughed; she had understood. And that is how I met Christos' Australian cousin.

"That's no witch," she laughed, and added in her distinct Aussie accent, "that's my aunt."

Nikki was as tickled as I to hear English. This cousin had grown up with Greek parents in Australia and had gone to Greece alone to discover her roots. She spoke perfect Greek, but was experiencing much the same culture shock I had on my first visit. We latched onto each other, talking and laughing all day. My sister-in-laws watched with smiles. They had never heard me talk so much and perhaps they were wondering if there weren't a bit more to their quiet American nifi, than they had thought.

Joanne and I emptied the wine bottle but our stories continued to flow as we made our way home in the dark, weaving from side to side under the watchful eyes of the stars.

A few days later, there was an incident for which my responsibility was clear but I was unable to defend my young nephew, Yeorgos who was unjustly punished by his mother, Anastasia. He was a high-energy tornado, whirling between the adults, kicking up dust and announcing his presence at every turn, which won him the reputation of *the child who probably did it*. If anyone said, "hey, stop it" from outside the range of our view, it would always be followed by Anastasia's high pitched, "Yeorgos!" as she reprimanded without further words.

So that Saturday, unaware that bread could only be purchased on weekdays. Joanne and I sat in the kitchen with the children around us while the bulk of the guests and relatives were in the yard, cleaning up after a feast, readying to nap as siesta time approached. I remember we were all laughing and whatever we were doing, entailed the ripping of the inside of a loaf of bread and leaving the crust behind. I was the major culprit, and very much enjoying the laughter and joy of the children.

Yeorgos was saying something and he grabbed the loaf from me and stuck his hand in the narrow, hollowed-out tube of crust. Just then, his mother entered and he froze, his arm in the air, a full loaf of bread pushed up to his elbow.

"Yeorgos!!!"

He broke into a run with Anastasia in pursuit—many more words following in rapid succession, of which none I understood.

"Linda, say something! Tell her!" Joanne was yelling at me, but mistakenly thought that I spoke fluent Greek.

I tried to get Anastasia's attention, but she was throwing words like bullets toward her son who had run upstairs and locked the door. His face was streaked with tears as he came to the window and the two exchanged a barrage of language, all incomprehensible to me.

"Linda!" Joanne was appalled that I was allowing Yeorgos to take the rap.

I grabbed Anastasia's arm, "I do," I said in Greek, pointing at myself and pantomiming my pulling bread apart; at least that was my intention. But it appeared by the escalation and increased pitch of her voice that she may have thought I was tattling.

I was able to get Yeorgos' forgiveness many years later, he remembering none of it as we laughed about it together. But on that day I felt sick with guilt and Joanne reprimanded me all evening—deservedly so. Not only had I let that small boy take my punishment, I had also destroyed the bread, the worst offense among people who knew of a time when there was not enough bread to feed their hunger.

CHAPTER 10

After little Fotis was born—finally, another son—Chevi's worst fears were realized. That summer the saplings on the farm fell limp over the dry and cracked earth. Rainless days were swept by the constant dry African winds. Chevi watched with dread as the signs emerged of a dismal harvest ahead, and she worried about the cries of hunger that she had always feared would come from her children, and that year they inevitably did come. Those cries would continue to haunt her as they echoed into her old age, long after hunger had left for good, which is the reason, years later she always kept piles of full flour sacks in the storeroom, sometimes in such a surplus that they fed only the mice in the summer and the mold in the winter.

But that dry summer there was not a surplus of anything— except hunger. Chevi had the foresight to send a message to her cousin in Kanali. The postmaster's wife was originally from Kanali, so when Chevi heard they were planning a trip there, she asked them to tell her cousin that she and her family were looking for a chance to pick beans when it was time to harvest them. She asked only to be paid in sacks of beans, no money. Such a deal had a better chance of being met with acceptance, as money was rare for everyone in the region and useless to Chevi, for Tomas would surely take the money for drink and leave them as hungry as they had come. Chevi knew her cousin would receive the message with the underlying desperation it brought and would be sure to find them work.

So that summer, Chevi and Tomas took their children to Kanali to pick beans. Baby Fotis rested in the sarmanitsa on Chevi's back while Anastasia, tethered to a tree in the field, played in the dirt. Tomas could read and write and therefore knew things such as where best to pick, and which tree's shade offered the best protection for his precious little daughter, Anastasia, to whom he insisted on attending throughout the hot days. Chevi showed four-year-old Eftihia how to hold open the sack while she, Vaso, and Niko plucked the ripened beans from their vines and shucked them from their pods, until her spine ached and the children's small fingertips turning white with calluses. When it was time to say goodbye to her cousin, they were paid with two giant sacks of beans, which were loaded onto the donkey to be taken back for the long hungry winter. But before they left, as Chevi kissed her cousin, she noticed someone had added a sack of rice and of flour to the donkey's back. She said nothing. She met her cousin's moist eyes in their silent acknowledgement of Chevi's unlucky fate in her father's choice for a son-in-law.

Back in Margariti, Chevi, in the company of Cochina, prepared for the long winter.

"My cousin writes from Germany with news of work," Cochina told Chevi.

The women sat by the well in the yard, braiding together onions to be hung in the cellar for later use. Cochina stood up and went to the fourno. She arranged pans of bread inside the large cement dome. It pushed a steady current of heat from its gaping black mouth and the red coals blinked at her from within. Cochina, had her kind tactful way, always trying to help Chevi, mindful of a person's dignity and a woman's limited choice.

"Cochos is talking about joining him," she said.

Cochina's cousin was one of many men from the area who worked in Germany, sent his pay home and afforded his wife and children—in addition to an income for adequate food and shelter—household goods that those without a person in Germany, could never acquire.

Germany.

To Chevi, it was a far off place that, until these past months, had been the villages of the invading soldiers of her youth, tall men with unsmiling faces and domes of metal on their heads, one of which would hang in the shack behind her house for generations, fascinating her grandchildren as they recognized the helmet from their history books. But for their yiayia, those Germans had come and terrorized the villagers, had eaten their sheep, their chickens, and their goats. Far worse than that—they had taken their olive oil, a guarantee of life, its nutrients and fat used as protection against starvation and they had left the people of the valley hungry. Those Germans had drunk the water from their wells, lived in their churches, shit on the graves of their loved ones, and then returned to Germany, leaving behind the smoldering houses they had set fire to and the lamenting cries from the widows and mothers of the dead. And now, twenty years later, Germany did not need to come to Margariti to take her sons, for she sent them willingly.

And Chevi, had noticed a different German invasion. At first it came in a trickle through the cracks of the isolated mountains and primitive roads of her valley, later becoming a flood as roads were paved and distances shortened by air travel. Those new Germans smiled at Chevi in Parga, as if they had been life-long friends, scaring the chickens as they sped by on motorbikes wearing floppy hats and dark glasses—you can't trust someone who wears dark glasses. They aimed cameras at her as she sold her goods in the market place and their young women shamefully showing their bodies, wearing nothing but underwear to swim in the sea, many of them leaving their breasts exposed, and the Greek boys there, gawking, with barely a thought that these were the people who had taken so much—the childhood of so many, the dreams of a generation. But there they were, swimming, drinking, dancing, as if the blood of Greeks had not been emptied onto these beaches by their fathers and uncles.

But Chevi also knew about this new opportunity in the place called Germany and now with five little mouths to feed, she needed to focus only on that.

"Nikos told me—did your Johnny mention to you? Theodore, you know, George's father? He went to the office in Igoumenitsa and wrote some papers for it—to work, to work in Germany."

Chevi helped Cocina move the loaves around with a long metal spatula, "And now he's going to Athens to see a doctor, then to Germany and work."

Her thoughts turned to Tomas. How could she put this idea in his head? With a long sigh, she imagined life, with a steady stream of products from this mysterious place. She knew from the stories that she had heard—few of which had been accurate, most having been pure fabrication or at best, gross embellishments of the truth—for if one were going to leave his village, his family, his entire life, for a far off place where people did not speak his language, to work from dawn until dusk in the closed air of a factory, then go to sleep in cramped quarters with burping, farting men from every corner of Greece, then one would make it seem a glamorous life, and who could blame him? They hauled back televisions with screens that showed only fuzzy white with a far off Italian voice, or bicycles with an inflated-tire-life of about a day on the steep inclines and the sharp rocky edges of the village paths. But mostly, Chevi longed for those precious monthly visits to the post office that she had seen the women who had men in Germany make—to collect that envelope with the blue paper that the postmaster recognized and changed to drachmas, which could be followed by a visit to the butcher, the grocer, the man who sells cloth. It was all there; she only needed to get Tomas there.

She sighed.

Cochina knew the hardship her childhood friend endured.

"We'll have a cup of coffee," she said pulling some hot coals to the front of the fourno. Spooning the pulverized coffee and some sugar into the water of the copper *brigi*, she held the long handle so the pot was positioned over the heat, stirring a few times, patiently coaxing the powder into a pungent elixir. The brown liquid rose to the brim swirling in pools of foam and before it could bubble to a boil, it was pulled from the heat and poured into the small cups, the frothiness sitting on top like the foam on a turbulent sea.

The women sipped their coffee and talked of superficial happenings of the village, but both knew the reason for this coffee. When it was finished, and turned upside down, the thick residue of the bottom, dripped into the saucer, creating a trusted window into the future with its drying patches of brown on the inside of the cup.

The two women, foreheads together, turned Chevi's cup over and looked inside.

"Money, Chevi" Cochina whispered and smiled at her friend.

"Money leaving me, not coming to me," Chevi answered quietly, contemplating, unsure. She was the more gifted one with *cafetzu*, having had so many of her readings come true with births and deaths and travels. Of course, the fact that those events are the most common of life even when not prophesied in the coffee grinds of one's cup was left unspoken, if it had been a passing thought. So Cochina pulled her head away, nodding silently for a moment, thinking, and then with her own interpretation she said, "Chevi, you are going to pay for something good, maybe."

"Ridiculous," thought Chevi. *"How can I pay if I have no money? And how can money leave if it is not here?"*

Then she saw it. "A road, Cochina. Here, look."

"Yes, you're right. Perhaps a road to Germany!"

Yes, Chevi saw a road. It was clearly a message that someone would travel. It was a long road, maybe a road to Germany but the end of it was closed off and that was very frightening. A closed road was not good.

A few days later, the village was abuzz with the news brought back by Theodore from his visit in Athens. He was not accepted to work in Germany. He had flat feet.

"Flat feet," Chevi thought, *"aren't they supposed to be flat?"*

The stigma settled over Theodore's house like a suffocating fog. He was not a real man. It was an embarrassment to the members at the café — though not applying at all for such work, did not seem to qualify for shame. He could not go to the Promised Land called Germany. His family would suffer and he could not stop it.

*   *   *   *

"Mama!" Nikos ran to the top of the stairs and flew through the doorway, "Did you hear?" He was out of breath. The news was ground breaking. None like this had ever been his to report.

"George's mother is going to Germany. She is working in

Germany. She's leaving next month."

Chevi stood under the grape vine that had grown up the side wall and settled on the exposed stone, creating a leafy roof over a small cement platform outside the bedroom. She knew and respected Katherine but she wondered, "What will she do with her children?" She continued poking the wood coals of the fourno that sat on the platform.

"Nikos, you must have heard wrong," she said, "George's mother has four children."

Nikos wiped the sweat from his eyes. "George's father is going to take care of them."

It was a simple idea.

Theodore was planning to do what no other man in Margariti ever had, or ever would afterwards, and he would never realize that his every act was carefully observed over those ten years that followed as he went about washing clothes at the spring with the other women, collecting wood on the mountainside and hauling it on his back, cooking daily meals and baking bread in the fourno, all tasks the women of the village were doing. And he was part of that group that also collected the blue paper at the post office — his wife conspicuously absent from the village events — but because of it, Nikos watched his friend, George, enjoy a fruitful life, while his own family descended further into poverty. Tomas and his buddies joked about *Mama Theodore*. But Nikos stored that memory and kept it safe for many years — that commitment George's father had for his family — Nikos would call upon it when he needed a model to guide him in his later life.

That afternoon, as Chevi heard this news, she wondered about being a working woman alone in a foreign place. Going there with another woman would make it less scandalous and much safer. She decided to pay Katherine a visit the next day. And when she left Katherine's house, she was determined to go with her the following month but first she needed a plan for the care of her children while she was gone.

*   *   *   *

The bus door opened and Chevi climbed down the stairs. Baby Fotis, his breath lightly falling on her neck, slept in the sarmanitsa on her back. Little Anastasia gripped her mother's hand as she jumped from the last step to the rocky dirt road below. The rest of the journey would be on foot, up the steep paths that no motor vehicle would attempt for many years.

A monologue played in Chevi's brain as she prepared her words for her mother-in-law — hoping she could convince the old woman to help her.

"When is the best time to approach her," Chevi wondered, *"perhaps in the morning."*

The ornery woman seemed to grow more hostile with each hour that was added to the day, which explained her father-in-law's disappearance as the evening approached, busying himself with some unnecessary task made to look necessary. Unlike most other men, he'd never visit the cafénio or taverna for that would present the worst of humiliations — as he had learned early in his marriage when she had come looking for him, screaming insults for all to hear, hitting him with a stick, kicking and spitting — too horrible to relive.

So Chevi climbed the mountain path slowly and when she arrived at dusk, her mother-in-law ordered her back out into the fading light — children still in tow — to collect water from the well and wood from the brush growing on the far side of the ravine. Returning with her load balanced between Anastasia on her hip and Fotis squirming between her shoulder blades, she was overcome with exhaustion. Chevi fed the children where they had fallen onto the sleeping mat, then curled beside them and slipped into a restless sleep, words swimming in her head, emerging in dreams of dark wooded ravines and wild animals.

In the morning, she approached the old woman before she could bark out new orders at her nifi.

"Mother-in-law, do you know why I am here?"

"No."

"I've come to ask for your help."

"Then, ask."

Chevi hesitated. She pulled her thoughts together, breathed in hard and then spilled the words from her lips, leaving them in a heap beside the old woman.

"Tomas does not work. Sometimes we don't even have bread. I go to my cousin for beans and wheat. My children are hungry. I want to go to Germany to work. I will work hard and send money. I will send money to you too." She ran out of breath.

Her mother-in-law was silent, waiting.

"Please, mother-in-law . . . if you could take these two little ones, I'll leave the older ones with Tomas and—"

"Are you crazy, Chevi?" Her mother-in-law looked at her in earnest. "I love my son. You took the best boy from me, but I know him and if you leave your children with him, they will die of starvation."

She watched the tears fill her nifi's eyes. "Go home. Tell your husband to go to Germany. It is his duty."

She was right. The coveted blue papers from the postmaster would not have the same meaning to Tomas as it would have for her. She could imagine him sitting in the taverna, buying drinks for every person who passed by and she could see the hungry eyes of Nikos, the sunken bellies of Vaso and little Eftihia. So that morning, without hesitation, she started back home.

Chevi reported his mother's message, but it fell on deaf ears. And for each time she brought it up, Tomas seemed to spend more time at the taverna. And that is where he was when The Man From The Bank came into the yard one afternoon as Chevi was drawing water from the well. Nikos and Vaso, with their neighborhood friends, had been running after the chickens and within the chaos Chevi almost did not recognize that there was a stranger among them. The Man From The Bank apologized for startling her as she scooped Anastasia off the ground, placing her on her hip in a protective stance. The sudden movement shook Fotis awake in the sarmanitsa and he started to cry. As the chickens squawked and ran in a frenzied circle, the children laughing and screaming, The Man From The Bank tried to collect his thoughts.

"Madam, I am here to inform you that," he took a deep breath and continued, his eyes darting around the yard as the children kicked up the dry dust, creating little clouds of haze along the ground, "the Bank of Greece has not had any payment for the lien on your home in quite some time, years in fact." The Man From The Bank cleared his throat and continued his rehearsed speech, raising his voice above the mayhem around him, "if payment is not made within the next sixty days, your home will be put up for auction and—" He hesitated. It became apparent that although there was more to this speech, he was changing course mid-sentence as he exhaled loudly and looked Chevi in the eyes.

"My dear woman, are these all your children?" He softened.

Chevi had not understood every word, but she had understood this person was a threat. So she fixed her black shawl around her, straightened her head scarf, and met the man's gaze with a smile.

"Yes, these are *all* my children," she answered.

"Listen." The Man From the Bank shook his head slowly. "I'm going to give you a piece of paper. You must give it to your husband." A thought occurred to him. "You *do* have a husband, don't you?"

"Oh yes." Chevi hesitated for a moment and then added, "But he is never here." She made a fist with her thumb pointed out toward her mouth, tilting her head back as if she were drinking. The man's face registered understanding and then disgust as he handed her a paper.

"Give this to your husband, and be sure he brings it to the town hall in Igoumenitsa as soon as he can. Do you understand?"

Chevi nodded. She realized then, without knowing why or how, that a great calamity had been averted. The man, having seen the children and the condition of the burned out home, had assessed the property to be nearly worthless which would allow them to pay a trivial fee, removing the lien and giving the master of the family complete ownership without debt to the bank.

But The Man From The Bank had seen many scenes such as this. He was grateful for a job with an income to feed his own family but to see this poverty, this desperation, was heartbreaking. He decided to stop in the town square to have a cool drink and to clear his mind, before his next encounter.

In the taverna, he gingerly sipped his orange soda, silently practicing his speech so as to have it flowing more professionally.

"George will think me incompetent," he thought.

He imagined the bank manager, the papers in his carrying case, and the conversation that they'd have when he returned to his office. He opened the bag, took out a folder and placed it open on the table. He read the directions to the next property. It was in that same village.

"*Past this taverna, up that embankment,*" he thought as he looked out the window and mapped a route in his head.

"*A warehouse.*" He wiped his brow. "*If it is unoccupied, I will —* "

"Orange soda, friend?" His thoughts were interrupted by the friendly voice at the next table.

"Come join me for an ouzo," said the stranger, with a smile and a beckoning wave. "It's on me. Tell me about your troubles. You look like a kind man with a difficult job."

Chevi was at the top of the stairs, just entering the front door when Tomas, his fist in the air and shouting obscenities, started up the dirt path of the yard, back from the taverna. He flew up the stairs and arrived in her path within seconds, shouting about the humiliation she had caused him. The children ran to the far edges of the yard to escape his wrath.

"How dare you talk to a strange man," he grabbed her arm, "and such lies! Such humiliation! You fool!" As he brought his hand up for the strike, cousin Miti's voice awoke him from his rage.

At the bottom of the stairs, in his warmest voice, he yelled up to his cousin's husband, "Tomas, how are you dear friend? Come and have a cup of coffee with me. Mitina has it in the pot as I speak."

Chevi brushed by them both and ran to Chavana's house, to visit with her friend for as long as she thought was necessary.

In the morning, Tomas took the bus to Igoumenitsa for business. He could read and write so he knew things and he was eager to tell all who would listen how he saved his home that day. Those who had been in the taverna when The Man From The Bank accosted Tomas with the humiliating insults—not being a real man, leaving his family to live in squalor, his children without shoes, his wife alone to face the poverty—chose not to bring that information into the forefront as Tomas told his saving-the-house story. But the humiliation remained and it was that which compelled him to look into the possibility of a job in Germany.

CHAPTER 11

In the summer of 1993, I still had one more year before I would have my bachelor's degree and could begin my gradual retreat from the restaurant life. That summer we would go to Greece with the expectation of buying a house in the heart of Margariti, inside the town square. Vangelis had called that winter. Nick told me about the conversation.

"He says there's an old house, only eight thousand dollars. It's small and it needs a lot of work."

A place of our own—I thought about it. In the U.S., we lived in my parent's house-apartment. I knew I'd never own anything. But a home in Greece? Did we dare?

"I don't know, Nick. Where will we get the money?"

We discussed a loan, but our credit was horrible. We were restaurant workers with low incomes, and this was long before the bank scandals of the new millennium where credit would be handed out like candy. We convinced my parents to take a loan on their house and worked out a payment plan. Then we prepared for our trip to Greece to become home owners. The thoughts of closing a door and having my own space or of having a bathroom inside the same dwelling where we slept, were such exciting ideas. So with the money in hand, we began the journey with our little second grader and fourth grader.

This was also the year when, a few weeks before, we had sat at the kitchen table, a letter signed by the school principal sitting on the flat surface between us, accusingly. We had discussed its contents—the strong recommendation for Nikki to go to summer school—neither of us quite sure of the weight a poor standardized test score could carry, and thus still able to foster an awe of learning in our children.

"We'll go to Greece instead," Nick had said, "and we'll show them history."

He was a firm believer in the Greek-cure for all ills, and given the choice of staying in the all too familiar grind of the sweltering summer kitchens or going to Margariti, it was an easy choice.

We stayed in Athens for a few days. Starting with a climb to the Parthenon, we walked around the Acropolis and the ancient Agora. We listened to stories about the Olympics while sitting in the Panatheniac Stadium, then investigated the artifacts in the Athenian Archaeological Museum, and afterwards examined the Temple of Olympian. We compared the attributes of Roman and Greek architecture while standing beneath the Arch of Hadrian, and ate our evening meals at the *plaka,* with the Acropolis lit in colored lights above us. We walked through history and spoon fed it to our children until their heads were full and their eyes glazed over. Then we began the trek north—the eight hour bus ride, snaking over hairpin turns, bouncing on the rutted road as the wheels smacked the pavement and our insides churned.

Weary, into our seventh hour, I thought I saw something up on the mountain top from the bus window, but I wasn't sure. It seemed to be a series of large white buildings. So a few days later, after we had settled into Margariti, we borrowed Fotis' car and found our way back to that turn in the road. Across the expanse of farms, as the greenness bent upward, there stood, on the edge of a mountain ridge jutting out through the trees, several large white structures made of marble—giant nondescript blocks of stone connected to each other at the top by thin appendages. They were about two-stories high and from the road they looked like what they were supposed to symbolize—women dancing in the traditional Greek steps. According to Nick, we were looking at the monument that had been constructed in memory of the women and children who had been trapped on the rim of that steep cliff, after having fled their enemy during the Souliote War of 1803, and they had chosen to dance off the edge, rather than be captured by the ensuing Turks.

I don't remember how we got up there. We must have driven, but I clearly remember standing with my neck craned, looking straight up at the massive structures.

I imagined being one of the fleeing women with my two small children, coming to that precipice and suddenly knowing that there would be no future. Then having to make that decision, in that time and in that place — the rawness of life and cruelty of war — incomprehensible to me, having been coddled in my twentieth century American world. Looking from Nikki to Thomas, as they listened intently to their father's story, my heart tightened and I felt my eyes blur with tears. A warm breeze swept my hair off my ears and I heard the women singing. They were next to me, hand in hand, the rhythmic movement of their legs kicking against the wool skirts, as their feet brushed over the ground.

"We will remember you," I whispered. "We will keep you alive."

*   *   *   *

Souli was a village high in the remote Pindus Mountains of Epirus. The Souliotes were tough people who were in constant conflict with Ali Pasha, the ruling Ottoman leader of that area. The European powers were interested in weakening the Ottoman power, so they encouraged those conflicts by providing the Souliotes with weapons and ammunition through the port of Parga. But in the winter of 1803, after much fighting, they were badly beaten by Ali Pasha's fighters. For their surrender, the oppressive ruler had promised them a safe retreat to the Ionian Islands — enough time to gather their possessions and then a departure without fear of harm. The Souliotes accepted the offer, though wary of their enemy's *promise*, and they began their journey to the coast.

Anastasia, a young girl of twelve, was among those in that retreat. Her last moments in her home had been spent wrapping food and possessions into a cloth, to be tied into a sling-like carrying case. In the rush, she had forgotten to take her jeweled head scarf, given to her by her yiayia. As she departed in the haste, she looked back, thinking to retrieve it but her mother pulled her along and there was only that last longing look. One last time, her eyes took in the familiar stone walls of the house, and the large almond tree that hung next to it brushing against the tiled roof on that windy day.

She followed closely at her mother's side as they made their way to the outer rim of the village, with thoughts of an uncertain future in a new home, for they were creatures of the mountains and to leave those peaks for the sea was troubling. Her stride was labored under the bundle slung across her back. And as they continued on, a shepherd from across the peak reached them breathlessly as they descended from the village square. He talked excitedly to the men, his arms waving, crying as he spoke—telling them of Ali Pasha's betrayal, the rapes, the mutilations—innocent blood spilled as the warriors carved a trail of mayhem in their advance toward Souli. The exodus became a frenzy of fear as the women fled with their children and the men prepared to defend them from the approaching fighters.

In their earlier preparation for retreat, Anastasia had known that she could take only what she could carry, and had put on every article of clothing she owned, but as they fled, it became a heavy burden and she fought to keep pace with the others. They climbed the heights and descended into ravines, only to climb again and again. And the moving mass heard death's approach in the echoes of the mountains as smoke began to billow above the peaks in the distance, but they kept moving. Over one mountain and then another. Small children on the backs of older ones. Tired, hungry, breathless, they pushed forward. There would be no rest.

Hours later, in the dim light of dawn, from the height of their position, they could see a band of moving horses and men approaching with a speed that could not be matched. They cried for their sons, their brothers, their husbands and continued their retreat, fear pushing them onward, knowing what had befallen those who had not escaped.

Suddenly, they came to a stop; the deadly ridge lay before them. Their mindless fleeing had trapped them high above a green valley with no hope for retreat. If there would be no escape for them, then death would be a kindness. There was no panic, no crying, only silence as the December wind came up the side of the cliff and called to them. One of the older women began to sing.

"Take my farewell little springs, forests and high peaks . . . "

And slowly, one by one, the others began.

"The fish cannot survive on land . . . "

"As the flower cannot survive in the sand . . ."

Connecting to each other with outstretched arms, the women slowly began to dance, *"and the Souliete women cannot live without freedom."* Arm in arm, they danced; babies bounced in sarmanitsas.

And then that older woman disappeared over the edge while the others continued with the smooth sound of their song.

And then one more was gone, and another.

Anastasia watched the edge grow closer. She did not understand that death awaited until her mother's hands grasped her tightly and she was hurling through the empty air, and then they were separated as the wind pulled them apart and Anastasia felt something — perhaps the branches of a pornari tree — dig deep into her forehead and the warm blood running into her eyes. Her body, encased in the layers of clothing, hit against rocks, down, down. Pain. Breathless. And then it was over.

Her back lay against the green grass. Her eyes, a warm liquid seeping into them, stared upward. They were lost in the blueness of the sky.

But she was alive!

Unable to move, she lay for some time, fighting for breath and slowly the air found passages to her lungs, filling her with strength as she pulled herself to her feet.

Chevi's great grandmother, Anastasia, would live her life and share her story!

Our drive back to Margariti was filled with questions from the children. They were just beginning, as was I, to understand the colorful history of their family. And it was that summer that I realized something about my father-in-law.

Tomas was a hoarder. He spent much time laboring over what Nick called *shacks*, which he built in different areas of the yard to keep his *stuff*. Each time an olive oil container was emptied, he would flattened it into a sheet of tin and squirrel it away. He dragged home random pieces of wood that he found on his walk to town or on the farm or among the olive trees. Nothing was thrown away: shards of metal, plastic containers, rusted nails and bolts, old roof tiles, broken tools. And when one shack was full, he'd start constructing another, which in itself was made from random junk like the rotten wooden shutters his children had replace on the little house which he had taken and stuck together with wire and tree branches to form a wall for one of the shacks.

The process infuriated Nick, as he watched the older man labor intensely in a way he had never seen him do when he and his siblings were growing up hungry and poor. It seemed that with each new improvement that the brothers and sisters attempted— the cement driveway and courtyard, the indoor kitchen and bathroom, the roof for the old house—Tomas would argue, hinder the labor, chase the workers away and then create yet another shack and fill it.

One day, at the onset of a rare passing summer rain, I scrambled to take cover in the little house with Nikki, Thomas, Marianna and Dina. As the giant drops began to splatter on the courtyard cement, Nick found his way to us. I sat with the children on an unkempt bed. The little house consisted only of two rooms, both being bedrooms. Nick paced restlessly, waiting for the rain to subside.

"There's no place for us to go," he mumbled.

I had been painfully aware of that fact from my first moments at the family house, nine years before, but I hadn't realized it was a frustration for him also.

He was also reeling from the disappointment, as was I, from the change in price for the house we had intended to buy. Someone had convinced the owner that the price was too low and he decided that he wanted double the money, pushing it out of our reach. Eventually the town would buy it and turn it into the Margariti Museum—a good use for it. But at that time, it was a great disappointment.

As the clouds parted for the returning sun, Nick walked briskly across the courtyard to the other house and instead of going into the front entrance that then led to the indoor kitchen, he opened the door next to it and attempted to enter the storeroom.

I had never given much thought to that door. It was a pest-eaten wooden door that scraped the ground noisily as it was pushed inward. Inside was a large rectangular windowless room with a dome-like ceiling. There were a few sacks of flour and some cans of olive oil but mostly it was filled with old wood, pieces of plastic and metal, broken shoes and an array of other useless items.

Nick stepped up onto the dirt floor, squeezed into the crowded room and began throwing items out into the courtyard.

"Come here. Help me." He motioned to the children and we all worked until we had a pile of junk in the courtyard and an empty storeroom. Fotis heard the commotion from the room above the kitchen that he had created for himself and he came down. He called his friend, Kolios to help. The three men worked with shovels to dig out the dirt floor, attempting to make it level with the other rooms.

At some point Tomas came home and saw the men working. Memories of the events as they happened that afternoon are a little murky, but the argument that ensued is as clear as the crystal sea.

Tomas began yelling and flailing his arms about. Nick met his father's words with the hot anger of crackling oil in a frying pan. The two were face to face — violent words passed between them. Fotis and Kolios retreated to the background as Nick continued spitting his fury, his father meeting it and throwing it back. The children stood and stared. My father-in-law was pointing at my husband, yelling, stomping his feet but Nick would not back off. After some long heart-pounding minutes, Tomas shook his fist at his eldest son, cursed his future and retreated up the stairs, his back to his children, disappearing through the old entrance. The air was electrified. Nick slowly turned toward me.

He winked, smiled, grabbed a shovel and disappeared into the storeroom. The two other men followed. Once the floor was level, Nick decided a window was needed, so he took a pick and began knocking large rocks from the middle of the stone wall.

"No, no, no, no. . ." Fotis came running over, "the room above is going to fall in."

Above the storeroom was the one room that remained from the original structure, the room that had not been destroyed by the fire and it was still piled high with possessions.

"You're weakening the structure." Fotis implored his older

brother to stop.

"Don't worry about it," Nick said as another blow landed on the wall, sending several large stones to the ground outside and creating a large opening that flooded the room with sunlight.

With a grin from ear to ear, Nick stood up in the opening and raised his two fingers high, showing a peace sign. I snapped a photo.

Poor Fotis. As was the habit in those days, Nick left the mess for him to clean up. We departed the following week for the U.S. and the cement truck was ordered a few days later. Fotis would oversee and pay for the new floor, the new window, the fresh paint and the furniture that would create a much-used living area for many years.

Tired and dirt-stained, Nick took a break from the digging. We sat together on the step outside the little house.

"Nick, what is this property here?" I pointed to the tangled overgrowth between the little house and the dirt road.

"What do you mean? It's just dirt."

"Well, is there enough room to build here?"

"Uh—" His eyes registered a hint of understanding. "Build?" He hesitated.

"Yeah." I continued. "Maybe we could add onto this little house. Make a bathroom—maybe a living room or kitchen."

He stood up slowly and walked to the metal fence, put his arms on the top and looked over the property—considering. He was nodding his head but said nothing. I stood next to him.

"So, what do you think?"

"Yes, it's a good idea," he said. "I'd have to get my father to split the property and give me this piece."

"Oh." That sounded like an impossible task.

"Don't worry. He'll cool off. Tomorrow, he'll be looking for money for ouzo or someone to pay for a taxi. He'll do it."

Tomas *did* split the property. He gave his two sons the houses and split some farm land between his daughters but Fotis would not find out that his name had not actually been put on the house—but only one half of the property—until ten years later when he would apply to the European Union for grant money that was being given to homeowners to create a tourist business— the house being used as proof that the applicant was serious about building and wouldn't just take the money and leave. But Fotis would be denied that opportunity, as he was told that he did not own that house on that property, but rather Tomas did. Tomas would refuse to sign the application, telling his son that he was saving him from debt. And Chevi would lose her last child as Fotis realized he would have to move away in order to make a life of some means.

But at that time, the children went to the lawyer's office in Igoumenitsa to sign the new deeds and they thought they understood the consequences. On the return bus, Vaso accompanied us back to Margariti.

"I need to talk to my sister. I'll be right back."

Nick moved into the seat ahead and the two talked for most of the ride home. Then Nick returned to my side.

"What was that about?" I asked him.

"I just wanted to be sure she was okay with the whole deal. You know, she helped me and my father build that little house. I told her she could have it, if she wanted. I would sign it over to her if she wanted it, but she said *no*."

I was relieved. I didn't want to alter our plans and I knew that Vaso did not like the village. Each time she came to rescue me when I was there alone, she would bring me back to her home and ask if I wanted to wash the village off of myself. She said it with a joking smile, but she seemed to feel Margariti was a place that she needed to escape from. Years later she would confront Nick, frustrated by some financial problems, and she would accuse him of being a neglectful brother, not having sent her the money that could have helped her, angry at having worthless Margariti farmland.

I had long ago, come to terms with my role in the U.S. as the wife of an immigrant, both of us uneducated. I knew I would never have the material life many of my peers were experiencing. Nick's family could not have understood how difficult it was for us to scrape together the meager funds we brought with us each visit. We were working long hard hours, and I could not justify leaving my children, to scrounge for money left on restaurant tables so that I could give it to someone else. At the end of each trip to Margariti, I would leave Nikki's clothes behind for Vaso's daughters because I knew that Nikki would outgrow them. I wanted to help in some way, but that was the best I could do at that time. Sadly, I realized that there were those people who had succumbed to the widely-believed myth of money-paved roads in America. We could not change that.

On the flight home, I looked out over the blue sky beyond the wing of the plane. I thought about all the changes that had occurred since my first visit in Margariti and the new living room that had been created on that visit. We also had our newly drawn architectural plans tucked away in a suitcase and the cement that had cost us the last of the eight thousand dollars would arrive in our absence and be used for a foundation for *our home* – giving Fotis one more job to oversee. And Nick would return off-season the following fall with more loan money, to begin the construction of the walls. I turned away from the small airplane window. I'd been wondering about something.

"Nick, how did you know the room above the storeroom wasn't going to collapse?"

"I didn't." He smiled. "I just didn't care if it did."

My husband – fearless and strong – when you have someone like that backing you, it's a little less scary to take chances. And that's how we were as I finished up my last year at the university and met the world with my degree the following summer.

Armed with a teaching license, I felt sure that I would get the job opening at the school in which I had done my student teaching. I had been a substitute teacher there for a few weeks when the new position opened. But I did not get the job, and I was devastated. I could have stayed there and made a living, as it was one of the highest paid substitute jobs in the area, but I wanted to teach, not babysit. So, I left.

It was a pivotal moment in my career and I found an unlikely mentor on my daily jog around my neighborhood. Sy Rubin, the father of Joanne's best friend, seemed to have the same walking routine as my running, and I would join him for a brief walk a few times a week. He had just retired from a long career in teaching.

"Are you sure you want to teach?!" He gave me his most sympathetic look.

I nodded.

"Teaching? Think about it. Are you sure?" He said the word *teaching* as if it were a cockroach.

I was sure. But I listened to what he told me and I acted on all his advice which would make a huge difference in my life and the lives of my family. He told me about one of his daughters who was a speech pathologist and he convinced me to apply for my Masters. I had just finished five years of school, and didn't know if I had the stamina but he pointed out that New York teachers needed a Masters anyway and it would be better to get something useful for when I realized that teaching was not what I wanted. So a few weeks later, I found myself enrolled in the prerequisite courses in the Speech Pathology Department at Hofstra University — my life signed away for many years on the loans that I would need. And one month after that, I got a call from my local school district. After a brief interview I started my new position as the high school ESL teacher. I would spend the next five years struggling with the uphill climb, through many tears and an arduous course load, working days at my new teaching position and once again, leaving my children while I was attending class at night.

My first day as a teacher was October 31, 1994. There had been no meetings, no mentors. I was given one textbook and thrown into the closet-sized ESL *classroom*. The students consisted of two Latino gang members, one angry pregnant fifteen-year-old, two silent Korean sisters, an extremely enthusiastic Ukrainian girl and three others who had no idea what anyone was saying. My years in the restaurants had not prepared me for much problem solving in that new environment. I had seen a stuffed trout sail past my head and land on a wall, the trout sliding to the floor while the crabmeat stuffing stayed glued to the wall for months, fist fights between grown men on the slippery wet kitchen floor as I walked gingerly around them trying to balance a tray, waitresses smacked by a hand in moments of anger for infractions such as dropping a tray full of glassware. The most valuable skill I had gained from those years, was to make myself invisible.

I wasn't quite sure how to approach the school administrators around me. I made many mistakes in those days and hurt people that I had not known I was hurting until I acquired enough experience to figure it out. I was so surprised to see how much work there was that didn't seem to have anything to do with teaching. When someone asked me what I thought of the whole thing, I remember answering truthfully.

"It's like marriage and having children. It's nothing like I thought it would be."

But when I walked down the hall of my school, I was hardly able to breathe from the pride that was choking me; I couldn't believe my good fortune—to be there—in a school, as a teacher, walking among some of my own former teachers. It was beyond wonderful and I was constantly fighting the lump in my throat that threatened tears as my elation won over my apprehension.

I was no longer able to work in the restaurant. My retreat was complete. And my income was cut in half. It was both painful and joyful.

CHAPTER 12

No one knew where Tomas worked or lived during his two year absence—not his children, not his wife, not even any of the Margariti workers in Germany. He had chosen to stay clear of the others and had gone further north to Nuremberg. He would never satisfy his curious children with much more than the information that Germany was a place that you had to stand at your job for hours and hours. And later questions of "What did you do at your work up there, Tomas?" would be met with sarcasm. "I danced all day!" or anger, "Work . . . I worked!" Whereas the other men always had stories and were eager to tell them.

In fact, the contract Tomas signed as a *Gastarbeiter* with the German machine manufacturer, called Siemens, committed him to work for two years and gave him a place to stay and a steady income of about twelve hundred marks a month, which was about seven hundred dollars or one hundred thousand Greek drachmas—of which only half would have allowed his family to live like royalty on the mountainside of Margariti, but alas, when Chevi went to the post office week after week, month after month, the postmaster always disappointed her, leaving her empty-handed until finally she stopped going and Markos' sympathetic eyes had told her, had he received anything for her at all, he would have run to her house to deliver it, personally.

Chevi worried about her children. They were hungry and she was afraid they would not grow properly. Nikos was away in Athens with Tomas' brother. He was going to high school there.

That meant that he no longer worked with Thansi on the road crews and brought her the extra money, but it also meant that he would be educated, like the Bakayannis boys. He would change the course of the Lykas bloodline. An educated man has many choices in life. Chevi could not have realized that on his return from Germany, Tomas would summon his son home from the foolishness of Athens to work the farm. Thus, sentencing him to a life of manual labor, which in later years would be far from home.

Vaso had already lost her chance for such an education. A few years before, the elementary school teacher had recommended she go to a prestigious boarding school in Athens to further her studies. The teacher had even sent the application and begun the procedures, knowing that a bright girl such as she would go far in such an environment. And after no response from the student's parents, the teacher had delivered the last paper to the house to get the signature for the eye exam—ready to escort the young girl to the doctor herself, if need be.

Tomas had been very personable, even a bit flirtatious—smiling graciously and making small talk as Vaso carried the coffee tray to the table under the tree. Her smile grew from the confidence brought to the yard with her teacher's authority. As they sipped from their cups, the teacher presented her case, Chevi—listening quietly—as her daughter's future was gingerly unfolded onto the table like a delicate lace cloth.

Tomas politely responded. "Thank you for coming by, Thaskala. We will certainly take it into consideration," He was a perfect gentleman.

"Sir, I would be happy to continue the procedure for you and escort Vaso to Igoumenitsa for the eye exam. I only need your signature." She smiled.

A bit more sternly, Tomas replied, "we will take care of it, thank you."

And when she had gone, Chevi watched helplessly as her daughter's hope drained in a steady flow like blood from an open vein and seeped into the dirt at her father's feet, Tomas exclaiming, "Athens!?! My daughter is no *putona*. Forget it!"

Vaso was as headstrong as her father, but a young girl's protests had no weight in that world. Tomas offered no further explanation, but Chevi suspected that her husband feared the possibility of losing his *workers*. It would be difficult to control his boys so he strove to secure the others—those who lacked autonomy.

So, it was her daughters Chevi worried most about. She knew well, the life they were destined for, there on the countryside. And it was these concerns that sparked a conversation in the Parga square with her friends from Senitsa as they sold their goods. One woman talked about her daughter in a government school right there in Parga. She was learning about sewing, weaving, needlepoint, housekeeping and household management. But most importantly, she lived at the school and was being well fed.

The following week, Chevi brought her eldest daughter to the school with gifts for the headmistress—a basket of eggs hanging from one arm and a live chicken clutched in the other.

Vaso's application was accepted and the following week with a few possessions, she left her home, not for a husband's home, but for a future. She would live at the school during the week and come home to help her mother on the weekends. And Chevi would see her each time she visited the market. Vaso had already been a reliable seamstress at her young age. It was known in Margariti that she was gifted with a needle and thread but at the school, she would fine tune that skill. Her teachers believed that she could be a top dressmaker and that she had a promising future with such a career.

As they became old enough, her sisters followed her to the same school. They would learn skills other than farming. They would choose their own husbands. They would create their own lives. Their freedom awaited. Sometimes, alone on the path to the farm, Chevi dreamed of their years ahead, and smiled.

*   *   *   *

Pavlos stopped his hand cart to watch the bus lumber down the mountainside, a cloud of dust following it. The metal groaned and whined as it rocked from side to side between the worn ruts of the dirt road. Tattered curtains swung within, following each jolt, revealing faces behind the dusty windows.

The bus' arrival in town was an honored event because the people of such a town where the bus would stop, were not an isolated backward bunch, rednecks on the peak of some desolate mountain, but rather a sophisticated people from within a valley so important and so sought after, as history had shown, that the bus stopped there—not once a month, not once a week—but every day! And that bus was no simple village-to-village bus, but rather The Athens Bus. It began its journey from the northern port of Igoumenitsa and arrived at its final destination, the city of the revered goddess, Athena, with stops only in important places—like Margariti.

Aliki with her two younger brothers jumped with excitement as they awaited its arrival at the side of the road, a low almond branch protecting them from the sun. They were eager to see what their mother had brought them back from Igoumenitsa and could barely contain themselves as the wheels squeaked to a halt.

"Mickey Mouse!" They jumped up and down with delight, clapping their hands as their mother emerged from the open doors holding up a comic book.

Pavlos smiled and was about to continue on his way, but as he grabbed the handles of the cart, another figure descended the bus stairs. There stood his friend, Tomas, back from that far off place—Germany. He dropped the cart and ran to Tomas, shook his hand vigorously while planting a loud kiss on each cheek and then a hearty slap on the back.

Tomas, eyes closed, drank in the aroma as the Margariti air embraced him: honeysuckle, thyme, wild oregano. He listened to the coos from the diving swallows as they rose and sank sharply through the air, and he watched them draw their half circles around him.

Home at last.

A deep sigh escaped as he exhaled. He was surprised at the joy he felt as his worn work boots landed in the dust on the road. He hungered to greet every villager, every animal, to pick up rocks and toss them into the air, to smell every flower, every weed. He scooped a handful of wild rosemary and crushed it in his fingers, bringing the fragments to his face and deeply inhaling.

The bus driver appeared and opened a large metal door on the side of the bus, revealing a storage area packed full. Tomas collected his belongings and with his friend at his side walked up the path toward his house.

"Well, well, look who it is," Mitina exclaimed, putting her watering can down as he passed her front gate; she walked out to greet him.

"What have you there?" She pointed to a bicycle perched on his shoulders.

"A gift for my son." Tomas puffed out his chest and continued his stride. Odysseus, the king, was returning to Ithaca.

As he continued on, more villagers joined the party as he relayed to them wonders of the great kingdom of Germany.

"Everyone has an automobile. And they are as big as three large donkeys put together. The roads are smooth and black. No stones! Not one."

"Ahhh, yes." They nodded their heads as if they could see the images he described.

He ascended the dirt hill to his house and was met with silence. No one was there. So what else could he do? He put his battered suitcase inside the entrance and hid the bicycle behind the well and headed to town for one small drink.

As darkness crept over the taverna window panes, Tomas became lost in time, telling and retelling stories of his long journey while providing an audience by way of a steady stream of ouzo, as was made clear to the proprietor upon his earlier arrival. But as night fell over the tiled rooftops, and his pockets grew lighter, he became eager to reacquaint himself with his wife, so he slowly made his way home, strengthened by the power of the drink, a victor, free at last from the toil of that far off land, back to claim his fair maiden.

Chevi stirred under the thick wool blanket when she heard the creaking floorboards. Tomas moved closer, his stocking feet remembering the worn wood with fondness. His bed on the opposite wall had been vacated upon his return. At the sight of his suitcase, Anastasia and Eftihia retreated to the cinderblock rooms at the foot of the stairs. But Tomas' interest lay in the bed occupied by his wife. He slowly undressed and slid under the thick wool, his hand searching for her.

Chevi rolled to face her husband.

"Your children cried for bread. I went to the post office every day until my shame would no longer allow it."

"I sent you money," Tomas whispered.

"I got two hundred marks."

"Yes, it was I who sent it."

"They cried for bread. They have no shoes. The girls do not have a proper dress for school."

"I sent you money." He reached out to touch her.

"Two hundred marks? Two years!" She sucked the air in short convulsive inhales.

"It was hard work, Chevi." His fingers tenderly felt her wet cheeks.

"You went there, so we could eat—"

"It was expensive to live there. It was hard. You don't know."

"The other men sent money." Her words came between muffled sobs. "Every month. Their women went to the butcher." Her face was pressed to the pillow, barely audible, "their children ate meat . . . two hundred marks!?" She turned her back to him.

Tomas swung his feet to the floor and slumped to the other side of the room, almost stepping on little Fotis asleep on a mat.

"You waste money." His voice was a wisp of air. The words held no power. "You don't know how to manage."

Chevi wiped her nose on her night dress and her muffled voice was lost in the cloth.

"You forgot us. You left me to take care of five hungry children." She breathed heavily into the dark. "You forgot us. . ."

Then there was silence. And the darkness choked them like the smoke of an accidental summer fire that ignites with a spark on the dry ground and ends with a charred mountainside.

CHAPTER 13

The passing of time was measured in our Margariti construction projects and our school years. In the summer of 1997, I was one year away from my graduate degree. Thomas would enter sixth grade in the fall and Nikki, eighth grade. Her struggle to decipher words and letters had reached an apex a few years before. In the spring of her fifth grade year, as she had been preparing to leave elementary school with a second grade reading level, I had finally come to terms with the need to have her tested for a learning disability. The teachers had tried every year to get me to sign the consent form—but my child was not *retarded*. She had recited the Greek alphabet at age two and by three could hear any information and explain it back: how satellites work, the pollination of flowers, photosynthesis! So how was it that she could not read? It had to be the teachers' fault. But slowly, through my own coursework, I began to understand how such a situation was possible. And if that knowledge had been mine at an earlier time, I might have destroyed my daughter's sense of her *self* with the inevitable parental fears that would have driven my actions, but instead I had thought it cute when she held the book upside down or made up words—my laughter making her smile. She was my first child, only the second grandchild of the sixteen my parents would accumulate in rapid succession, and we didn't have a measuring stick of experience. But as time progressed and I began to write her name in the margins of my textbooks, studying about specific reading problems, identifying behaviors that I recognized were common for her, I began to understand and I focused all my energy into learning all I could on how to help her. In the meantime, Thomas, who had been able to read since kindergarten and would gobble a book, such as the *Hobbit* in a matter of days, who could write complex thoughts and understand inferences beyond his age, began to do all he could to get the attention of parents who seemed to be everywhere, except with him.

It was also the year that my parents decided that they wanted to sell the house and move to Florida. We didn't want to uproot the children; they would have enough to adjust to with the sudden absence of their grandparents, Thomas being especially close to my father who was a dominant figure in his life. I remember at Thomas' kindergarten screening when a young woman had read him four words: chair, sofa, bed, father—and then asked him which did not belong. He answered correctly: *chair*, for he had seen his father sleeping on the sofa or in bed, but rarely upright in a chair. It was my father who spent time with him, nurturing him as he had done with his own six children.

So Nikki and Thomas watched their grandparents pack their possessions and we adults worked out a plan for the purchase of the home, accepting higher mortgage payments for the extra money that would get us to Margariti that year and add to the construction. My parents headed off to Florida with a moving van as Nick and I moved our family onto the larger side of the house. And it would take some years for my siblings to realize it was not *mom and dad's* home anymore.

That summer, we boarded the plane, all four of us, taking a respite from the chaos we called home, and we started our journey—once again on our way to Margariti. As we walked to our seats, an odd feeling chilled me. Something was sucking the oxygen from the cabin and the aisles pushed inward. The warm air became oppressive heat. Beads of sweat trickled off my neck into my blouse as I stumbled to my seat, confused by the racing of my heart. Staring down at the floor, I trying to focus, to calm myself—hoping it would pass.

"Mom, what's the matter?" I wasn't sure which child was speaking.

"Shhh. Sit over here." It was Nick's voice, and then to me he said, "What's wrong?"

"Nothing. I'm okay." It slowly passed.

It was the first *episode* of something that would occur at random moments for the next several years and then would subside as life became more manageable.

That trip, however, did not offer the rest we had hoped for. It was the *year of the plumbing*. The plumber was a young man from the village and we would receive a phone call from him in the U.S. ten years later, apologizing for his behavior. But that summer we had not yet learned that friends from the village were usually not the best candidates for seeing a job through with professionalism. And we didn't want to cause any hard feelings within the family for not using a friend of an uncle or a cousin's son-in-law, but the money for these projects was so hard to come by, eventually we would find it necessary to seek out those workers who were the most interested in their professional reputation enough so as to provide an appropriate work ethic, something that was common among the Greek American immigrants that I knew from the U. S. but seemed to be more elusive to their brethren at home.

So every morning, rather than pack for the beach and begin a day of fun, we waited for Nick as he drove Fotis' car to the plumber's house after he failed to show up at the designated time. Nick would have coffee with the young man's mother as she tried to rouse him from his half drunken stupor after his early morning return from the bouzoukis. Then we would have to sit and wait for him to do his job, for if we left him to work independently, as we found out on his first day of the job, he would disappear moments after we had left. The ten-day plumbing job took over a month and required *beach days* to be replaced by many *village days*. It was not one of my fondest summers in Margariti.

*   *   *   *

Two years later, in the summer of 1999, having finally received my graduate degree the year before, I was finishing up my *Clinical Fellowship Year* as a speech pathologist – a requirement for certification with the American Speech and Hearing Association.

For me it would by eighteen months instead of twelve because my teaching job had limited my ability to fulfill the required hours, so I had been working after school, evenings, weekends, and holidays—extending the twelve months, to eighteen—which also meant that I would have to spend that particular summer in an office attending to patients. So that year, Nick and the kids left me behind, to travel to Germany and meet up with Fotis who was living there at the time. They would drive south to Italy and then take a ferry across the Ionian Sea, to the port in Igoumenitsa.

According to one of the many tales the kids brought back, Nick and his brother drove through the night to make it to the Italy-Igoumenitsa ferry, so Nikki and Thomas were asleep in the back seat when they parked the car into the tightly packed hull of the ship and went atop for coffee! Thomas was the first to wake up as the water rocked the vessel back and forth, churning his stomach and he—not knowing where else to do it—opened the window and vomited down the side of the car. Then he pulled himself through the front window, as the cars were too tightly packed to open a door, and he ascended the stairs to look for Nick and Fotis. Nikki awoke soon after and encountered the same issue with the doors, so she slid herself out the window, her sandals in her hand, and she felt her feet push down into a warm slimy liquid on the floor, which was also dripping down the car door. Both children were eventually reunited with their uncle and father.

"Oh they were fine," Nick defended himself, "we were just at the top of the stairs. We could see the car."

But I wasn't sure he could see anything when he was engrossed in one of his conversations with his brother.

That was the *year of the eaves*. Nick had drawn up an ornate, multi layered design that would create the cement eaves, in preparation for the roof that would eventually be built on top.

"We don't do it that way, here," the mason told him.

"I didn't ask that." He was tired of hearing objections on every leg of the project. "Can *you* do it or should I find someone else?"

"Well, I can do it, but it won't look good."

"That's my problem, isn't it?"

When it was done, it looked fantastic and even more beautiful with a roof on it the following year. The kids had the video camera, which would provide me with a window into their activities. And when they returned a month later, I would enjoy it tremendously as they, with their cousins, performed on the screen, walking through the maze of walls, sunlight pouring over the new eaves, and for the first time I would realize that the years of labor and sacrifice were actually going to bare fruit. I saw a house emerging in the blur of bricks and cement.

*   *   *   *

The following summer, the millennial year, we all went to Germany, borrowed Fotis' car, drove down through Italy and spent two days exploring Venice. Then, we took the ferry across to Igoumenitsa. Armed with money from another mortgage and feeling confident that we would be able to make the exorbitant payments, we sought out a reliable roofer.

Nick had a very specific plan for the roof that required much reinforcement with treated beams, which is the plan that The Roofer From Senitsa agreed to follow. It had been necessary to remove the old roof of the little house, which had been absorbed into the new house the year before when the eaves were constructed, making it necessary that summer for us to stay elsewhere. We took residence in the living room which was the former store room in the old house. The beds were lined up, our suitcases and possessions piled around the room.

It's not a pleasant situation to sleep in the same room as your adolescent children. In addition to our having different sleep patterns, noisy night breathing, and a variety of bed squeaks, there was no screen on the only window, so it was kept closed all night to avoid mosquitoes. The stuffy air made for headaches and irritability.

The circumstance was bearable only because we had expected The Roofer From Senitsa to begin construction soon and when it was done, we'd be able to move back into the rooms of the little house. But he didn't show up and time passed. Nick sought him out and talked to him again, and he promised to begin within a few days, but a few days turned to weeks and then we questioned whether The Roofer From Senitsa would ever begin.

"Don't worry," he reassured us, "I'll work on it when you've left and you'll have a perfect roof when you come back."

That's when Nick realized what was happening and with a few choice words, he told The Roofer From Senitsa what he could *do to himself,* and fired him. But I was baffled.

"What's going on?"

Nick explained. "This guy is waiting for us to leave so he can do the job when we go home—when no one's here to see what he's doing. He wants the money and then he'll probably use fewer beams, probably not the quality I want. Without me or my brother here to watch how he's building it, he could pretty much do whatever he wants."

Eftihia told her brothers of a quality roofer she knew in Igoumenitsa, but he didn't drive. He would need a ride back and forth every day.

There were only eleven days left and although The Igoumenitsa Roofer had a son-in-law who worked with him, two single workers would not be able to finish in that time. Nick and Fotis would have to help. Eventually, we would all help by carrying the roof tiles up the ladder, handing them tools, bringing them water. The work was started early every morning. Chevi would cook a large midday meal which we all would stop to eat, but no one would take a siesta—including the neighbors, though they had no choice in the matter—and after ten days, the roof was finished, one day before our departure. Chevi, in keeping with the old traditions, insisted on affixing a wooden cross to the roof with a clean towel hanging from one end and some apples from the other. This was to show that the final step in making the structure a true home—the completion of the roof—had been accomplished. The cross, a symbol of a Christian home, was something of importance to a woman who rarely visited her church but was ingrained with memories of a time when one's religion determined survival. The towel was a message to all who viewed it that this was a family who respected its workers, thus providing a towel for their use, and the apples symbolized a fruitful future for the inhabitants of the home.

The *year of the roof* left us exhausted, and it was time to go back to a schedule more grueling than any in the past. The bitter taste of that summer kept me away for several years, while Nick took some off-season visits to see his mother and to install windows and screens in the house.

*   *   *   *

In the fall of 2004, with both children in college, Nick and I were experiencing a second honeymoon. Life had never been so good. He tried to convince me to return to Margariti, but I could not shake the memories of the past. And why would I want to leave Long Island then? We finally had a comfortable income and time alone to enjoy it. In the end, there was a compromise. I said I'd go, but only for three weeks.

So after a five year absence, in the summer of 2005, I accompanied Nick to Margariti. When we arrived, we entered our cement shell and closed the door behind us. It was filled with the loose cement-dust that we created with every step. The exposed bricks had holes for spiders and centipedes that I would battle during our stay. Without ceilings, our voices echoed up to the exposed roof tiles that were draped with webs. A porcelain toilet was affixed to the floor in the empty cement bathroom and rocked back and forth when it was sat on. A shower head with its exposed pipes was propped up in the cement wall.

It was glorious!

There were screens on the windows, efficient plumbing, a small washing machine, one bed and a lock on the front door. It was the first time, since our visit as newlyweds, that we were there without kids—ours kids or the sisters'—and it was a far different experience than it had been that first time, an eternity ago.

It was so wonderful, I didn't want to leave. I learned what it meant to relax and regenerate. And, except for the year that Nikki would get married, we would return every summer.

*   *   *   *

The following summer, 2006, Nikki had just graduated from Albany University and Thomas was in his second year at Binghamton. I had my teaching job and per diem work as a speech pathologist, which gave Nick the ability to make his departure from the restaurants at his leisure, but as it turns out, when one is not drowning in the whirlpool of survival, one's job can be a tolerable task, so he continued to work—an aging man at a young man's pace. On the other hand, I found myself alone on the weekends and wondered what all the toil had been for. I thought we had fought that twenty year battle so that we could be together. But, Nick said he didn't feel comfortable not working when I had two jobs, so he found a five-day-a-week job as a cook at a local diner, with Sunday and Monday off.

That was the summer that Nikki and Thomas returned as adults to Margariti with their father, the first time since the *year of the roof*. That visit reconnected them to their childhood memories—remembering themselves as villagers among friends and family while also enjoying the comforts provided by the new house. After a short while, they returned to Athens and the three met my arriving airplane at the airport. We spent the day sightseeing and reminiscing about our old days in Athens. Then the kids boarded a plane to return to New York as Nick and I made the drive north in Fotis' car.

Three weeks later, we went back down to Athens and greeted my brother, Bob, his wife, Anne, and their three daughters. They had decided to visit Margariti after having heard so much about it for so long. We spent a few days with them in Athens showing them the sights and then we rented a car for the drive north. Nick drove ahead in Fotis' car with two nieces and I drove in the back seat of Anne and Bob's rented car with another niece, ensuring that they never felt neglected.

I sat leaning forward. My head protruded through the bucket-seat space into the front of the car, separating my brother and his wife. I provided a steady monologue, describing the scenery and little anecdotes that came to my mind as we drove on the winding road through beautifully sculptured mountains and over rough terrain, and we chose the nicest places to stop and eat, and steered them toward the tastiest Greek cuisine, and when we arrived in Margariti, we settled them into our beautiful new home, where I

was so proud to offer a place to sleep — almost free from insects —
complete with screens and a washing machine, and then we
showed them a different beach each day, because the topography
surrounding the area was the most exquisite in the world and we
didn't want them to miss any of it, and we discussed what we had
done that day, going over the details of each step, never leaving
them to feel lonely or neglected, as that would be a terrible insult.

And then I saw it.

The day before we would escort them on the drive back south
for their departure, they were coming into the house and my
sister-in-law looked up at me. Our eyes locked for a split second,
and there it was. So clear! How had I missed it in all those days?

My transformation into a Margaritian had been so gradual, I'd
never realized it was happening and by then it was so complete, I
had become blinded by my love for the place. But at that one
moment, I had recognized that look. And I knew. She was *me* . . .
the old *me*. The American *me*. The anxiety that comes from the
strangeness of a new culture was there in her eyes. She needed the
privacy of which I'd been depriving her, the choices she had been
denied, and I looked around the house and saw the dust, the
cracked cement, unfinished fixtures, hanging wires, and complete
lack of anywhere to sit and relax, except for the beds in the
bedrooms.

The weariness in those eyes, I knew it well.

"No, no, no," Anne would say, as she read my book, "I did
enjoy myself. Really."

And I would tell her, "Yes, I know, but it was mostly a difficult
trip. I get it. Let's move on . . ."

*   *   *   *

In the summer of 2010 Nikki came back to Margariti for a short
visit. While there, she accompanied Nick and me to a cousin's
wedding. When she got up to dance a traditional Greek dance —
basically the only artifact left from her eight years in Friday-night-
Greek-school, our table exploded with applause.

"Bravo, Nikki!" They were so impressed to see the American

girl keeping step with the other Greek dancers.

"Who is that?" Elias asked Chevi.

"Nikos' daughter."

"What? No way!" He looked to the young woman dancing and back at Chevi. "It can't be. I am looking at you Chevi. Her face. Her smile. That's you!"

Elias was the son of Uncle Spyros. He stood to watch my daughter and his gaze was far off. He saw Cousin Chevi, the young woman he remembered as a small boy growing up in the village.

Chevi beamed. Yes, she knew it. She had thought the same. It was an incredible experience to see herself again as a young person. And that *young Chevi* — Nikki — Nikos' daughter, could read and write. Chevi had heard about the school she was attending then. Imagine that — she'd soon be a doctor! And her brother, little Thomooli, a lawyer! The dream Chevi had dreamt for her own children was still alive, hers to watch unfold within that new generation. She felt the pride of her ancestors rise in her. The Lykas bloodline, her blood, would prosper in her children's children. Chevi watched her granddaughter, her legs sweeping in the rhythm of the music as she turned with the other dancers. She thought of her other grandchildren.

And she smiled.

CHAPTER 14

Tomas had ordered his younger brother to send Nikos back from Athens. There was a farm that needed to be worked and so Chevi would have her oldest child home in Margariti again. With no other choice, Nikos returned but he would never be able to reconcile with the fact that the man who had abandoned them for two years, a person he saw as an irresponsible nitwit, was able to make such a sweeping decision that others adhered to. That fact, coupled with the increase in the boy's height, created a steely stubbornness between them, like two rams with locked horns. And Chevi watched helplessly as her son spent a few months in Margariti and then returned alone to Athens—a boy of fourteen. He would take the bus back once in a while and give her some money that he had earned from working at odd jobs and then he would disappear, presumably back to Athens.

In fact, Nikos would leave Margariti and head to the neighboring villages near the sea with some spending money he had left for himself. At fourteen, he had reached the physical height and build that he would carry to adulthood and that fact aided him in his search for *fun* as he and the friends he met along the way spent time entertaining the young female tourists, drinking and dancing in the discos at night, camping on the beach, and hanging around the cafenios in the daytime until the money was gone—except for the price of a bus ticket to Athens. It was on that directionless path that Nikos spent his young years, until mandatory military service at the age of nineteen.

During Nikos' frequent absences, Tomas focused his fury on his wife, his daughters and his younger son. But the other children shared their older brother's anger and argued with their father often. After losing her chance for school in Athens, Vaso had talked to Eftihia of ways they could get into nursing school. As their departure from the Parga school approached, they looked into possibilities for applying to a nursing program. But they learned that they would need their father's permission and Tomas was not going to give up his daughters, not to school, not to marriage.

Vaso was able to get a job in the purse maker's shop in Margariti, but when she heard of the factory jobs in Plateria, just a short bus ride away, she applied for herself and her sisters. Anastasia would soon finish in the Parga school and at the age of sixteen begin cleaning hotels, but Eftihia would join Vaso on the twenty minute bus ride each morning when their applications were accepted to the factory, and they would help their mother with the household expenses bringing some financial relief that Tomas would also enjoy—much the way the pot is watered with the flower.

In 1981, Vaso would hear of a factory job in Filiates, an hour bus ride from Margariti. She would apply for herself and her sisters.

"Filiates?!" Tomas was livid, "I won't let you go!"

"We're not asking you," Vaso remained calm.

"I won't allow it. If I have to tie you up and beat you. . ."

He had never hit his daughters and Vaso knew he was clutching in desperation to any threat that might intimidate them into staying, but they found strength in their three-ness.

"If you touch us, I will go to the police and have you arrested,"

Tomas was silenced. Defeated.

The three sisters would move to Filiates and live in an apartment together and each would fall in love and marry. None would ever come back to live in the village. But when the police officer in the black car came to Margariti, they were all still attending school in Parga.

The black car rumbled to a stop at the end of the driveway and Chevi came slowly down the stone steps, holding the stone wall of the house for support, hardly able to breathe. Her imagination conjured up horror at the sight of the police officer walking up the dirt path to the house. There had been no word from Nikos since the letter six months before. She made it to the bottom step as the stranger walked into the courtyard.

"Is this the home of Nikolaos Katsiotas?" he asked without a proper greeting, his stern brow set in a scowl as he looked around the yard.

"Who are you?"

"I am here to serve a subpoena on behalf of Olympic Shipping."

He loomed over the small woman and extended his hand.

"What do you want?" She kept her hands at her side.

"I want to speak to Nikolaos."

"He's not here."

The stranger pulled some papers from a folder. "This paper shows that Olympic Shipping is suing . . ." He hesitated, pulled some glasses from his shirt pocket and held the paper up. "Nikolaos Katsiotas to recover the fine they paid to, uh . . . the U.S. office of immigration when he abandoned his post as third engineer on the Olympic Freedom, on February 20, 1978, in Brooklyn, New York."

"Huh?" Chevi's quizzical look broke the business-like demeanor of the stranger just as Miti walked up the dirt path—the black car having produced much conjecture among the neighbors.

"Chevi! Good morning." His smile further thawed the business exterior of the police officer and the two men talked amiably for a while. Then the stranger turned and left Miti holding the paper that had been presented to Chevi.

Miti explained the situation to Chevi. Then he looked at the paper and whistled.

"Whew, they want two thousand dollars from him. If he tries to come back, they'll probably stop him at the airport." Two thousand dollars which translated to seven hundred thousand drachmas may as well have been a million. It was more money than any of them had, but Chevi knew that her son was in America, a place where gold coins laid in the street and one only needed to bend down to retrieve them.

This was the longest she had been separated from her son. It was a common occurrence for the mothers of Margariti to have their sons live and work in Germany, and then see them on holidays or summers, but America . . . would she ever see him again?

Chevi put her hand to her heart. She felt pain deep within, a pain that brought longing, a pain that narrowed her throat, making it hard to swallow. Why hadn't he contacted anyone?

"I want to call him," she said.

She knew Miti had a phone in his house.

"Do you know the number?" Miti asked.

"It's in New York. We'll call New York . . . the post office. Surely they'll know where he is, or they'll give him a message when they see him."

Miti thought to explain it to her, but then said, "What did his letter tell you. Was there no phone number? We need a number, Chevi"

She shook her head slowly, "he's with Tomas' cousins. They are in New York. That's all I know."

"Go get the letter. Let me look at it." Miti knew that Chevi would not have been able to read it, so maybe Tomas had missed something.

Chevi produced the letter from her apron pocket and Miti read its short contents.

"Hmm . . . no phone number, but he is working at a restaurant."

Chevi nodded. She knew that information. What she didn't know was that on the February afternoon that the police officer had mentioned, her son had stood with his shipmate, Spyros, watching from the deck as the ship glided gracefully into Hudson Bay, approaching the Brooklyn harbor. Ahead, the Manhattan skyline jutted up from the water's surface like blocks of glistening golden in the setting sunlight and to the left, a massive Statue of Liberty stood silhouetted against the violet horizon. And Spyros, the adrenaline shooting into his bloodstream and clogging the pathways to the part of his brain that plans ahead, decided at that moment that he would stay there—in New York—and that he would dock with the Olympic Freedom for the last time before embarking on the road to his fortune in America! But he lacked the courage to do it alone or to discuss his idea with his friend, Nikos.

The two young men were among the thousands of young Greeks of that era who became seamen in order to make a viable living. The avenues for village boys such as themselves were few, and the shipping industry offered the healthy able-bodied ones an escape from the monotony of the village, while at the same time providing a much needed income for their families. There was also the underlying expectation of *seeing the world*, when mostly they would only see the world of harbors and ports. But it was an *exit* and they used it as their first step in escaping the poverty of the village.

Upon their arrival in New York, the men had been at sea for two months straight. Nikos would get his shore pass from the immigration officer who would come on board after they docked and would deem him to be low risk for *jumping ship*. He would get his spending money for the nightclub, from the second captain. At the end of his service with that company, it would be deducted from his pay, an amount that would be calculated based on the contract he had signed and the sum left after half was sent home to Margariti each month.

When he had returned from his first experience at sea, a few years before, he had changed the automatic pay deductions, which had been his entire pay—every penny of it sent home to Margariti each month. He wished there were a way to get it to his mother, directly, but like all else in her world, it had to pass through Tomas first. He could read and write so he knew what to do with letters from the postmaster. Nikos had gone sixteen month without shore leave, without any pay for himself, eating only the food provided and buying the occasion carton of cigarettes. He had his entire pay sent to his mother. But in that fourteen months Chevi had seen none of it! Never even knew it had been sent and Nikos had returned to his home to see it in the same squalor he had left. And if his father had been grateful for that sudden monthly windfall, he had never expressed it.

So on his following trip, he had taken his full pay, no deductions to be sent home. He would return to Margariti with a lump sum and hand it to his mother. But that ship's route between South America and Europe had brought him to so many beautiful ports where he had enjoyed the nightlife and culture of each—so much so, that when it came time to return to Margariti, he had nothing to bring his mother. He spent a week in the village, acutely aware that *flat-broke* was how his father had returned from Germany, and then he boarded the bus to Athens. Destination: the port of Piraeus. It was a place that offered consistency, where one could reliably find a new ship and even get an advance on one's pay. That is where he signed away his freedom for nine months with a new contract on a new ship.

So with those two failed attempts at trying to get some money to Chevi, he decided to send half his pay back to Margariti and he hoped some would make it to his mother. And it did — in small drips, but it was enough for her to pay for bread and items at the market.

Nikos stood with his friend on the deck, surveying the New York skyline. Spyros stood silently as The Olympic Freedom slid toward the port under the watchful eyes of Lady Liberty. Then he turned and looked at Nikos.

"Let's get a shore pass."

A few hours later he was nudging Nikos toward the bow.

"Hurry up, I want to get to the club before midnight."

They had their dollars as they descended down the gangplank in Brooklyn, New York on that February night in 1978. The icy air hit their faces as the two men hailed a cab.

Greek seamen knew they could find a little piece of home in every seaport, tucked close to shore. They were always expected by the Greek restaurateurs, bouzouki nightclub owners, Greek food shops, and welcoming women. Nikos had been to ports in the U.S. several times but this was his first stop in New York.

"Where to?" The taxi driver turned to the two men and though none of the three quite understood the other's broken English, they knew the routine and Spyros needed only to say the name of the Greek nightclub where they would spend the hours drinking Chivas Regal and listening to bouzouki.

Around two in the morning, they headed back into the unfamiliar cold to return to the ship. As they approached the harbor, Spyros slowed his pace.

"Listen Nikos," He looked at his friend sheepishly, "the ship is gone."

Nikos stopped walking. "The ship leaves at five. What are you talking about?"

"No," Spyros looked down at the sidewalk, kicked a few pebbles with his foot, and shoved his hands in his coat pockets. "It left at one. The captain changed the time." His words were turned to frosty wisps of air as he spoke.

"What?" Standing in the frozen grayness of the streetlights, within the fog of too much scotch, Nikos wasn't quite sure what his friend was saying.

"Man, what are you talking about? We missed it? Okay then." He fished in his wallet for the number to call the ship as he looked around for a telephone booth. "I'll call. It's okay."

The men needed only to call the ship and airline tickets would be waiting for them at the nearest airport to bring them to the next port, which on that night would have been somewhere in Texas. It sometimes happened that ships were missed.

"No wait." Spyros put his hand on his friend's shoulder. "I have a cousin here. We can stay with him. I have his address."

"Stay? Here?" Nikos looked toward the docks. He could see flashes of the black water reflecting the night sky from between the port buildings.

The sea.

It promised timelessness—without beginning or end. Though the navigators change as the centuries pass, the sea stays constant, always there. Reliable. Something Nikos yearned for. As a sailor, his movement was dictated by his vessel, its body submerged in those waters of time. He could walk from stern to bow, but the destination was set by the compass whose direction was well defined—the metal tip pointing to its course with precision—reliability.

But if one should move that metal tip ever so slightly, only a micro-millimeter to the right or left, the direction would change. And it would not be a significant change over the first few meters, but it would become monumental over time as the angle of trajectory widened with every movement forward. And as time passed with the rolling of each wave, the distance from the original intended destination would be immense—impossible to breach in the time allotted for the journey.

Spyros sensed his friend's uncertainly and repeated, "We'll go to my cousin's. He has a house. We can stay with him." And before Nikos could answer, he felt his friend's hand on his shoulder, "It's America, Nikos . . . New York!" And no further explanation was necessary.

So Nikos decided to stay and see America. And with that decision, the direction of his journey changed ever so slightly.

Spyros took his cousin's address from his wallet. The men showed it to some stray patrons leaving the Greek nightclubs and armed with that new direction they headed to the train.

It was in a place called Astoria, Queens which looked much like Brooklyn. The train took them into the sky above the roads. There were many signs written in Greek; Greek flags hung from storefronts and apartment balconies. The train doors opened and closed at different corners on the elevated track, and the passengers were speaking Greek. As the two young men climbed the stairs to a second floor apartment, the familiar smells of oregano and rosemary wafted from the dark corners of the hallway.

This was America?

Spyros' cousin, eyes swollen with sleep, opened the door to his *house* and the two young men walked into a small studio apartment, the mattress of an unmade bed inches from the doorway. There was a small closet-sized galley kitchen with dishes piled in the sink and boxes of food piled on the small square surface of a counter. A door next to the waist-tall refrigerator was pulled opened and a woman emerged from the bathroom. Spyros' cousin introduced his girlfriend. She did not speak Greek.

"Do you know anyone in New York?" the cousin asked Nikos. It was not an invitation to stay.

Nikos remembered a phone number his father had given him, a cousin—but they had never met. He pulled it from his wallet. The cousin took the paper, turned to his girlfriend and said a few words. She gave him a few coins and he disappeared out the door, returning a few minutes later with news for Nikos.

"Someone is coming to get you. Here, have a seat." Then he turned to his girlfriend and rattled off more words of which Nikos only understood, "coffee."

A small table was pulled to the bed and the three sat awkwardly together on the edge of the mattress as the girlfriend tinkered in the *kitchen* a few inches away.

After some time, there was a knock on the door and the cousin greeted the *someone* who was there to bring Nikos to his cousin. Spyros quickly wrote his own cousin's address on a small scrap of paper torn from a napkin and his family's phone number in Greece, on the island of Corfu. His smile was tired.

"Contact me as soon as you can," he said, "we'll go out to bouzouki." Then he kissed Nikos on both cheeks.

The two men never saw each other again.

Nikos left with the person who had come for him. He was brought to an apartment close by and told that his cousin was coming to get him but it would take a little time.

Inside the apartment, he was heartily greeted by a group of Greek men playing cards, a pile of dollars in the middle of the table, their heads clouded by smoke. One of the players had a fat cigar hanging between his lips. He looked up at the young Greek and laughed.

"You're in America boy!" He pointed to the money. "Here you can have all the money you want! Women? . . . You want women? You can have all of those you want too!" He let out another long hearty laugh and the others joined him. And Nikos decided he would stay a little while and see what it was all about.

His cousin finally arrived, Cousin Nikos—they had the same name—and Cousin Nikos drove him away from the city. The buildings grew smaller in the square mirror on the side of the car as they drove at a high speed on an empty highway toward the light that was just beginning to turn the sky a subdued pink.

And the direction of the compass needle was reset.

His cousin lived in a big house in a town called, Hicksville. His wife greeted Nikos warmly and a small boy peeked shyly from behind her. Nikos slept until midday and then his cousin brought him to his restaurant—a diner, thirty minutes away.

He found more cousins there, the brothers of that one, and other Greeks from Northern Epirus. They sat in a large dining room at a table with white tablecloths that had red cloth napkins folded into smooth triangle. Nikos was served fish without bones, and fresh salads and vegetables, and warm fruit pie with American coffee. It was a delicious meal coupled with sweet conversation about the villages and life in America. His cousins offered him a job and a place to stay and Nikos saw it as an opportunity to see that wonderful new place called Long Island.

That afternoon, Nikos was brought to the house of Mrs. Elleni in a town called Smithtown. She was an older Greek widow and she rented rooms to some of the young Greeks in that area. That became Nikos' new home. His new job would start the day after.

"Washing dishes?" Nikos thought of the small cafes back home, the small sinks with suds and greasy plates, "How bad could that be?"

The next day he was brought back to the diner and put behind a mountain of dirty dishes, the size of which he'd never seen, and it grew larger as the frenzy of waitresses circulated in and out of the swinging door – their angry faces shouting words at him that he could not understand. His instincts told him to leave, quietly find the back door and disappear to freedom. But how? Instead he watched the small Latino man beside him and then picked up a dish with one hand and the hot water hose with the other. And that was the America he saw for many months, but he knew it would only be temporary. He would never stay in such a place as that *Long Island* — Margariti was his home.

In the meantime, Chevi thought of her son and stopped by the post office often. But there were no more letters. She tried to distract herself and decided to finally go to Chavana's house to see that new television her husband had brought from Germany. She sat with her neighbor watching a snowy picture on a square screen.

"Look at this," Chavana's husband showed them how the round dial could change the picture several times. Then on the screen, Chevi saw a ship being tossed by waves in a storm.

"Stop." She held up her hand to the man, "let me see this."

"Are you looking for your son?" He laughed at her. The waves were taller than the ship and it was being tossed onto its side. "Nikos is in a ship like that . . . and maybe he's going to drown in the sea!" Chavana's husband slapped his leg and bellowed with laughter at his cleverness.

Chevi stood up with a start, her coffee cup falling to the floor, "You're a donkey's ass." She rushed from the house, tears starting down her face.

That night, as she lay restlessly turning under the sheets, she saw her son. He was a small boy of ten or eleven, being tossed among the waves, choking on water.

"Mama!"

She bolted upright in her bed, wet with perspiration, dawn just breaking through the window.

"Tomas!" She woke her husband, "Tomas—you must go to your cousin. Get a phone number for his brothers' restaurant."

Tomas was barely awake. From across the room, he sat up.

"What are you talking about?"

"Nikos . . . I want to talk to my son. I need a number."

"Oh leave me alone. He's fine. He's a big boy."

"Tomas, please."

He was getting out of bed, "okay, okay. I'll take care of it."

So Chevi tended to the two sheep that her Grandmother had given her, to ease the loneliness that grew with each step of independence her children took, and Chevi felt a little lighter knowing that she'd be able to hear her son's voice soon.

In the evening, as Tomas stumbled up the driveway, Chevi was eager to meet him.

"Well?" She waited.

"Well what?" His expression was blank.

"The phone number?"

"Oh that . . . I'll take care of it . . . I'll take care of it." And he climbed the stone stairs and disappeared through the entrance.

In the morning Chevi waited at the bus stop. She knew the village's name. It was near the town of her husband. As she entered the bus, the line of people stopped behind her.

"Do you know the village, Krania?" She asked the bus driver.

"It's not this bus. You need the Athens bus and then switch to—"

Chevi backed off the bus steps.

"Athens bus," she whispered to herself, "Athens . . ."

She chatted with passersby as she waited for the next bus. When it came, she climbed aboard and asked the young man behind the wheel, "is this the Athens bus?"

"That's what it says, yiayia." He pointed to the sign above his head.

"I'm going to Krania," she said.

The driver looked at her. "Yeah. Okay. Take a seat." An older man, with the ticket book in his hand, followed her to her seat.

"Madam, be sure you get off at Louros." He helped her to her seat as the bus lurched forward. He smiled. "Is someone meeting you there?"

No." Chevi settled next to the window, her head leaning on the dusty glass. The bus wound around mountains and through local villages and each time it stopped, Chevi looked to the ticket writer, questioningly, and he clicked his tongue and raised his head to indicate, *no*. But finally, she heard him call to her.

"Madam, this is Louros."

The bus to Krania was much like the one before it, until it began the snaking climb to the top of a mountain, back and forth, up the incline where it deposited Chevi in a village square. It was clear to the inhabitants that this was a stranger and she quickly identified herself as the wife of a cousin.

As it happened, the other Nikos was visiting from America.

"What luck," Chevi thought, *"this was surely someone who would have the number."* He was one of the restaurant owners. She was quickly led to him, and Chevi, after appropriate greetings, stated her case.

Cousin Nikos frowned. "Sorry, I cannot help you." He had never met this woman, did not know why her son had decided to go to America, and did not know if his cousin in America would want to be found. With a sense of what felt like loyalty, he hesitated, "uh, I don't have the number. Don't worry. Your son will—" but he wasn't able to finish.

"What!?" Chevi pulled at the ends of her head scarf. "You have it! Give it to me!" Tears began to fill her eyes. He was saying something but it was indecipherable through her angry cries.

"What kind of a man are you? Not giving a poor mother her son's number."

"Calm down, calm down. Let me—"

"Don't *you* have a mother?" Chevi cried.

People began to gather.

"What does she want? What's happening here?"

Cousin Nikos heard the grumbling around him.

"Okay, okay." He took out a piece of paper and wrote something on it and Chevi plunged it deep into her apron pocket.

She wiped her eyes with her scarf. "When is the next bus?"

"Would you like to stay? You can sleep in my home, or just

come and rest a while. Visit with my mother. Have a cup of coffee."

"No thank you. When is the next bus?" Chevi could think only of the phone call she wanted to make.

"Please stay. It's late."

"I can't. Tomas will worry." She lied. "The next bus?"

Cousin Nikos decided to drive her to Louros and he waited with her until he saw that she was safely back on a bus.

It was dark, late evening when she finally returned to Margariti, but she made her way to Miti's house. She would not rest until she heard her son's voice.

Miti took the paper. He dialed the phone, waited a few seconds and then hung up.

"What!?" Chevi's patience had disappeared hours ago.

"Cousin, I think it's early in the morning there. No one answers. Come tomorrow morning. We'll try again then."

She stood there motionless, not wanting to wait until morning, not wanting to face the night without reassurance.

"The time is different there Chevi. It's okay. We'll call in the morning."

With a sigh, she turned and left.

At dawn, Miti opened his shutters to find his cousin sitting under the grape arbor. He dialed the phone, waited, and spoke into the receiver.

"Hello," he spoke in Greek. Apparently the person who had answered, understood. He talked for a minute, with Chevi straining to hear the other voice, and then he handed her the phone.

She took the receiver and screamed into the phone as if to breach the distance.

"Nikos, it's me. Are you okay? What are you doing? When are you coming back?" She gave him no time to answer, but she heard America in the background—dishes clanking, people talking.

At that moment, I was behind a counter, a young *waitress-in-training*, cleaning up after the lunch rush, making coffee, stocking cups and silverware. And a blond, golden-skinned Greek, having been summoned from the kitchen, was at the front desk talking loudly into a phone receiver in a language I did not understand.

"Oh, who's that?" I asked the woman who was training me.

"One of their cousins." She shook her head. "Stay away from him," she warned. "He's trouble."

"Hmm." I looked over at him and found him watching me. His steely green eyes pierced mine.

And my heart began to thump.

A FEW LAST WORDS

Chevi took her last breath on July 5, 2013 after suffering a stroke three weeks prior. She lay comfortably in her own bed in Margariti with all of her children nearby. Nick and I had arrived two weeks before, but Chevi never saw the finished book or knew that her story would be told. I was too late.

Though her world was small, and her resources limited, Chevi was a woman of great strength. She quietly fought against a rigid patriarchal society and she won. More than anything, she wanted her children to be happy and her daughters to be free.

And they are.

ABOUT THE AUTHOR

Linda Fagioli-Katsiotas lives on Long Island with her husband, Nick. She teaches English to newly immigrated English language learners at her local school district.

She has also written a novel, *Your Own Kind*, a love story of yearning and desire, of the basic need to connect with others and the expectations of culture and tradition that sometimes keep us from real love.

You can visit her at: www.truestorythenifi.blogspot.com

16414650R00088

Printed in Great Britain
by Amazon